Directions for ministering to hurting people.

Emotional wounds are difficult to heal. That's why Rita Bennett offers a practical approach to dealing with emotional hurts. In **How to Pray for Inner Healing for Yourself and Others,** she provides basic training for ministering to the needs of emotionally distressed people through prayer counseling. With the many techniques and prayer helps she gives, you can encourage others to open up to the Holy Spirit, gain God's perspective on their own problems, and forgive those who have offended them.

Topics Rita covers include:
- Preparation for counseling
- Working with a partner
- Forgiveness prayer
- Reliving troubled memories by picturing Jesus in the scene
- Prayer for healing prenatal emotional wounds
- Prayer helps for specific emotional traumas

BY Rita Bennett

Emotionally Free
I'm Glad You Asked That
How to Pray for Inner Healing for Yourself and Others

How to Pray for Inner Healing for Yourself and Others

Rita Bennett

Power Books

Fleming H. Revell Company
Old Tappan, New Jersey

Library of Congress Cataloging in Publication Data

Bennett, Rita.
 How to pray for inner healing for yourself and others.

 Bibliography: p.
 1. Prayer. 2. Spiritual healing. I. Title.
BV227.B46 1983   248.3′2   83-10981
ISBN 0-8007-5126-4

TO
Shade O'Driscoll and Janet Biggart
my first two prayer partners,
and the growing number of brothers and sisters in Christ
who selflessly give their time and lives
praying for the wounded, brokenhearted, the bruised,
restoring sight to the blind

Contents

Introduction

This book is written to show people how to help themselves and others receive soul healing from Jesus through prayer. I want to express my own confidence in what Rita is telling about. I am myself receiving healing that is letting the light of Jesus into the dark places in my own personality, and changing some basic attitudes in a way that amazes me!

I had a secure childhood, with loving parents, but nevertheless sustained serious hurts, and acquired a great many fears that have dogged me through life. My mother was severely handicapped with arthritis, and unable to give me the physical affection I needed, although she was everything a mother could be in other ways. My father was a pastor—a warm, impulsive man—but although I knew he loved me, he almost never showed approval of me or of what I was doing.

I spent my first three school years in England under the old brutal system of discipline (read Dickens, you'll get the idea, although my experience wasn't *quite* that bad!). When I was nine, my dad moved us to the USA, and I experienced the culture shock that might be expected. Added to all this, until I was fourteen, I was always the "runt" of the group! At any rate, I developed a highly negative and fearful attitude toward life, with some real hang-ups.

Receiving Jesus helped immeasurably, of course, and later, when I was baptized in the Holy Spirit, I thought all of my problems were settled! And of course they were, as long as I walked in the Spirit. I soon found, though, that that was hard to do. My *spirit* was just fine—joined to the Lord, and seated with Christ in heavenly places. But my *soul* was still stuffed with things that needed correcting and healing. By the Baptism in the Spirit, the Lord was able to take care of some of them, but the deepest hurts were firmly repressed, until I began to pray for soul healing.

As I see Jesus in past situations, and let Him heal my feelings, I am experiencing startling changes. I used to be apprehensive about the future; now I find myself looking forward with joy. Most important, I am experiencing an increase in spiritual freedom. As my soul is healed, I find I feel more love for the Lord, and more confidence that He loves me. And I believe I am going to receive even more help as I go along.

There are many scriptural examples of soul healing, but there is one clear passage in the Book of James:

"Confess your faults one to another, and pray one for another, that ye may be healed" (5:16). That's the King James Version. Modern translations usually read, "Confess your sins one to another. . . ."

The usual word for *sin* in the New Testament Greek documents is *hamartia*. But James here uses the word *paraptoma*. This word is used as a synonym for *hamartia* in a number of places in the New Testament, but it may also be translated *fault,* and this is the way the King James translators chose to render it. It seems pretty clear why. (Scholars will note that the translators of the King James Version would have been using the older Greek manuscripts, probably the so-called *Textus Receptus.* The later manuscripts do not have *paraptoma* here, but the more common *hamartia.*) This passage speaks of confessing to one another. You don't confess your *sins* one to another; you confess them to God. You may confess them in the presence of your pastor or another person, so he can assure you of God's forgiveness, and pray for you. You may ask another person to forgive you for what you've done to him, but you confess your sin to *God.*

Then, too, the passage speaks of confessing in order to be *healed.* But you pray for sin to be *forgiven,* not *healed.* And this is why, I believe, the KJV translators chose the word *fault.*

A fault is a defect. An earthquake fault is a break in the earth's crust. It does no harm in itself, until it slips! Then you can have widespread destruction. Similarly, a defect in the human personality is a fault, not a sin. If you have a hot temper, that's a fault. You can't help it. You got it from your ancestors, or from your childhood experiences. Just *having* a hot temper isn't a sin, but *losing* your temper is. If you lose your temper, you'll have to confess your sin and ask that it be forgiven, but you also need to pray that the hot temper—the fault—will be healed. If the fault is healed, the sin is avoided. I think this is what James is talking about, and it's what we're doing in inner-healing prayer.

It's not much good to tell someone to try harder unless you offer help to heal his faults. Then he can begin to ascend to what we might call a "beneficial spiral" (the opposite of a *vicious* spiral!). If my hot-tempered friend loses his cool, he needs to confess his sin, and be forgiven. If he's permitted a spirit from the enemy to control him through his temper, he may need to bind and cast out that spirit. He is now ready for inner healing, for the fault of weakness of bad temper to be cured. Then he needs to cooperate with God by trying to behave himself. If he fails again, he takes another turn around the spiral—confession of sin, forgiveness, deliverance, healing, discipline—but each time he comes out higher up, and gradually the bad temper is cured, and the sin no longer occurs.

I am eager to recommend soul-healing prayer to you. It's not really new, but it is finally coming to the fore in this present day as the most recent truth being restored to the Christian community.

Rita has a way of presenting this truth so that it is highly understandable and usable. People everywhere, both in leadership and in private life, will benefit by reading this book and applying its teachings.

It really works. It's exciting. Don't pass it by!

In the love of Jesus,
DENNIS BENNETT

... pray
for one another,
that ye
may be healed.

James 5:16 KJV

How to Pray for Inner Healing
for Yourself and Others

Thou shalt guide me with thy counsel. . . .
Psalms 73:24 KJV

1
What's in It for You?

Dear friend, you are reading this book either because you're already involved in soul-healing or inner-healing prayer and would like to learn more, or because you think you would like to get involved. Perhaps you need healing yourself, or you're concerned about guiding your family to wholeness—your neighbors, your community or—who knows—the whole human race! Congratulations on your decision. The world has been waiting for you! A pastor friend once said, "It's going to take all that all of us can do to do God's big task." God has a calling for each one of us. Perhaps this is one for you. I highly commend it.

If someone had cared enough and known how to help Lee Harvey Oswald, the tragedy of President Kennedy's untimely death could have been averted. Oswald's background, movingly told in psychologist Dr. James Dobson's book *Hide or Seek*, shows how he was rejected from his earliest days right up to the final chapter of his unhappy life. "When he was thirteen years old, a school psychologist commented that he probably didn't even know the meaning of the word 'love'." How many people are there like that in the world you touch, dying for someone to reach out to them, care about them, pray for the healing of their souls? How many others would be protected from hurts (and worse) inflicted from that wounded person?

Perhaps you will be able to help even one such person. Maybe the people around you aren't as needy as Oswald was, but God can heal all levels of hurt, large and small, from the time of conception and birth, through childhood, teen years, adulthood, right up through old age.

Some Background on This Ministry

I've been involved in the healing ministry since 1961 but since 1977 I have been especially interested in soul or inner healing. More and more churches are recognizing the need in this area and are inviting their people to participate.

In 1978, Dennis and I began presenting what we call "Healing of the Whole Person Seminars," teaching and ministering wholeness for spirit and body, but also, in a deeper measure than before, *for the soul.*

The seminars began in our own church; then we were asked to share them with other churches of our own and other denominations. We now conduct some twenty-five seminars each year in many parts of the country, and in other parts of the world.

We don't do all the praying at these seminars. We teach people how to pray for one another. This way, after the seminar, participants aren't left waiting helplessly until the next teacher comes along. They are prepared to continue the work of prayer-counseling themselves, having received some training and experience, and gained confidence by it. And it's working! We regularly hear from churches and individuals that the ministry is continuing, even though it may have been two or three years or more since we were with them. This is exciting!

Why This Book Was Written

The idea for this present book came from preparing counselors to pray for people at these seminars. We normally hold a four-hour training session for those who wish to help pray with others. Obviously, one cannot teach everything that needs to be taught in those four hours. I felt the need for something people could read ahead of time, and use as a text, not only at our seminars, but anywhere there is interest in this kind of ministry.

Here and there in the book you will find material in brackets and italicized. These "asides" are mainly for those preparing to be prayer-counselors at a seminar. Others can skip over them, or may find them helpful.

How to Pray for Inner Healing is also written for those called to a continuing soul-healing prayer ministry, and to help pastors and other leaders know how to guide people who are developing this ministry. Pastors and laypersons need one another and need to know how to help one another.

In this book, I am sharing with you what God has taught me, as I have talked and prayed many hundreds of hours with needy, hurting people. I'm not going to simply give you surface material. Even though I won't be able to spend hours of time with you myself in prayer experience, I'm going to give you as much detail as I can to assist you and the prayer partner or partners you will work with. (By the way, there's great value in working in twos, and I will be telling you more about that later in this book.)

My own background was in education and child welfare. I also taught retarded children and worked with emotionally disturbed youngsters. I've been the wife of an Episcopal clergyman since 1966, so I understand something of the needs of churches and church groups. I directed this ministry in my own church for the three years of 1978–1981, pioneering the work there. I have taught prayer-counselors in numerous churches of various denominations in the United States and other countries where we've held seminars. I know what soul-healing prayer ministry can mean.

This book doesn't claim to give all the acceptable or possible ways of praying. As clearly as I can, I've given you some pages from my own experience; you can go on from there. It's a rewarding ministry.

May I emphasize to you at the outset that this present book is a sequel to my book *Emotionally Free,* which is a one-volume, basic-resource book on the subject of inner healing. Much that is said in this present book will be based on the teachings in *Emotionally Free,* and I will refer to it from time to time. If you haven't already done so, it's important that you read it, in order to understand clearly and receive the best help possible from this present work. I hope you will also read others of the many good books on soul healing that are available today. You will find recommended reading in the Bibliography.

The Originator of Soul Healing

The Originator of inner healing or soul healing was Jesus Christ Himself. He began healing broken souls and mending broken hearts nearly two thousand years ago. When on earth Jesus said, *"He [my Father] has sent me to heal the brokenhearted,* to preach deliverance to the captives, and recovery of sight to the blind, *to set at liberty those who are bruised . . ."* (Luke 4:18, paraphrased). But Jesus also said, "Most assuredly, I say to you, he who believes in Me, the works that I do he will do also . . ." (John 14:12). There isn't any hurt in life—no matter how terrible it is—which can't be healed by Jesus. By the power of the Holy Spirit, Jesus will teach you, and move through you, His modern-day disciple, as you follow Him in this ministry.

> He came to touch people
> at the very core of their beings
> and to love them to wholeness.
> He's showing you and me
> how we can do the same.

Who has directed the Spirit of the Lord,
Or as His counselor has taught Him?

Isaiah 40:13

2
A Starting Point

There are three areas in a human being: spirit, soul, and body, and each area has its own needs.

The spirit is the part of you that makes you human. It is the image of God in you that is able to respond to God. When you receive Jesus as Savior, the Holy Spirit comes to live in your spirit. From then on, though your soul and body may be relating to the earth, your spirit is in fellowship with God in heavenly places (Ephesians 2:6).

Your soul is the psychological part of you, made up of emotions, will, and intellect. The third part, the body, is the physical part through which you contact the world in which you live.

The *soul* is the part of you that is in most need of healing. Your *spirit* was completely healed when you invited Jesus into your life. (I am assuming you have received Jesus as your Savior and Lord. If not, please do. *See* Appendix 1.) Through Him the Holy Spirit came to be joined to your spirit, and you received the gift of heavenly life—you became a new creature in Christ. As you pray for healing for the other parts of your being, always remember your *spirit,* the central and core part of you, is *whole.* What can cause distress to your spirit is to reject what God's Spirit shows you is right, and begin to walk on your own, *away* from the life and love of Jesus.

Your soul or *psyche* is composed of not only your conscious mind but also the vast area of the subconscious. (By the way, many interesting things are continuing to be discovered about the human brain; for example, the recent research being done on hemispheric dominance. Some studies sound as though the brain *is* the soul, but the soul, but we need to realize that the brain is not the soul. It is part of the physical body and dies when the body dies. As Doctor Howard Dueker, a neurosurgeon friend of mine, puts it, the brain is the machinery of the soul but not the soul.) The needs of the soul, both conscious and unconscious, have often been overlooked by Christians, who assume that rebirth of the spirit has taken care of everything. This is because the soul has so often not been distinguished from the spirit; therefore the terms *soul* and *spirit* have been used interchangeably. This great need for healing of the soul is being increasingly and dramatically recognized today. A Christian can live most of his life psychologically injured or debilitated, die, and go to heaven—but how much better to pray for healing and be a part of the cure rather than a part of the sickness of the world! (For fuller understanding of spirit, soul, and body, read *Trinity of Man* by Dennis and Rita Bennett.)

We have recognized rightly our need to confess our sins against God, and against others. Jesus died on the cross so that we could be forgiven, but *we* need to learn how to forgive at a deeper level.

Most of your soul hurts are caused by the sins of others against you and your own reactions to those sins. Sometimes these sins of others are accidental and sometimes purposeful. Sometimes accidents and other results of the Fall of man, such as disease and death, are the cause of soul hurts. Unless your reactions to mistreatment are sinful, then these soul problems do not affect your relationship with God.

Some Other Important Observations as We Begin

We are talking here about healing the soul, but not overlooking or forgetting that the spirit, soul, and body are all interrelated and affect one another.

The term *inner healing* is being used widely today and in various ways. Most of the time it's used to refer to the kind of Christian soul-healing prayer I am talking about. Since the term *soul healing* may be new to some, I'm using both terms as I go along. What I want to emphasize to you at the start is that I'm talking about *Christian* inner healing, and that *Jesus* is the One to whom I am directing you in healing prayer. He is the only Savior. Also, my focus is on *Jesus Christ,* the Healer, and secondarily *ourselves*—not the other way around.

I want to emphasize, too, that I am *not* giving a short course in psychological counseling! What is taught in this book is not do-it-yourself psychology. If I pray for someone who is physically sick, and he gets healed by the love and power of Jesus, I am not practicing medicine. Similarly, if I pray for someone who has soul problems—who is mentally or emotionally sick—and Jesus heals him, I am not practicing psychology or psychiatry.

In this book, we are looking at mankind's nature, his dilemma, and his cure, as it is presented to us in the Bible. Truths from psychological and other sources are accepted and applied, when they are in agreement with the Scriptures.

There is a desperate need for people's souls to be healed. The main obstacles to the Spirit of God's moving with power through people are the hurts in their souls. It is the continuation of Jesus' saving work in a vital and overlooked area. It isn't going to be done just by a small group of highly trained professionals, but by willing people who learn to pray for one another effectively. Only in such a way can the vast need be met.

What Is Soul-Healing Prayer?

My favorite definition of soul-healing prayer is:

> Teaching people to practice or accept the presence of Jesus in their past, present, and future—helping them to forgive everyone and setting them free to live in the present at their fullest potential.

So I will be talking to you about specific prayers for the past, the present, and even prayers for the future.

My husband, Dennis, says it this way:

> Inner healing is simply cooperating with the Lord to let Him cure and remove from our psychological natures the things that are blocking the flow of the Holy Spirit.

This soul-healing ministry does *not* take the place of psychologists, psychiatrists, marriage and family counselors, and the like, any more than spiritual healing of the body makes doctors of medicine unnecessary. This isn't because God is not willing to heal everything, but because we human beings are often limited in our ability to receive God's healing. (If someone feels led to seek help from professionals, he or she should try to find those with the best skill and education possible who are also committed Christians, filled with and led by the Holy Spirit. If a Christian is not available, a non-Christian may be chosen, provided he or she will not try to tamper with or undermine the faith of the counselee.)

We use the term *prayer-counseling* but it's much more *prayer* than *counseling*. If counsel is given, it should be by inspiration of the great Counselor, Jesus Christ. As a counselor, you will lead people to The Counselor. In the work of inner healing, you will be looking for avenues of prayer and receiving spiritual gifts with which to heal the hurting, rather than confronting, or giving advice.

Why Is This Kind of Prayer Needed?

I want to strike an encouraging note here at the very beginning. Every believer has already received some inner healing because:

> Every experience with Jesus
> brings inner healing.

However, a Christian, even one who is a recognized leader, may still have great need for inner healing. What are the things he or she may need to cope with? Here are a few: poor self-identity; self-hatred; feeling God doesn't love him or her; hatred of others; unforgiveness of self or others; self-aggrandizement; self-centeredness; bad temper; a hypercritical attitude; embarrassment from a physical, emotional or mental handicap; loneliness; rejection; depression; persecution; divorce; false guilt; various sexual problems.

There may be yet unhealed needs from the death of someone close and dear; from being in or causing an accident; from fears or memories of pregnancy and giving birth; from memories of own prenatal hurts, or birth trauma; or from being an unwanted child.

As we said, soul hurts mainly come from things others have done to us. Here are examples: incest, rape, spouse's unfaithfulness, an alcoholic parent or mate, and all types of unkind treatment during life—too numerous to enumerate completely.

Purposes of Soul-Healing Ministry

Again, the purpose of soul healing is to make us able to follow in Jesus' steps and help others do so.

"You shall love the Lord your God with all your heart [center of your life], soul [intellect, will, emotions both conscious and subconscious], mind [psychological and physical], and strength [body and soul]. This is the first and great commandment, and the second is similar. You shall love your neighbor as you love yourself" (Luke 10:27 and Matthew 22:38, 39 combined and paraphrased by author). Although we know God our Father through Jesus His Son, all of us want to grow in a closer relationship to Him. Until healed, some people feel closer to the Father only, or to the Son only, or perhaps to the Holy Spirit. We need to grow in our love of God in His *Triune* fullness.

Then, too, you need freedom to love and accept yourself, or you certainly won't be able to love your neighbor. Of course, Jesus isn't speaking of narcissistic, self-centered love when He refers to your loving yourself. The love He means is centered in Him, and through Him we can love ourselves properly for the first time. The Rev. John Powell, S.J., says in *The Secret of Staying in Love,* "There is no doubt in my mind that a deep understanding of and a serious effort to achieve true love of self is the beginning of all human growth and happiness."

We love ourselves because He first loved us.

We need to be able to restore and deepen relationships with our neighbors. Jesus didn't mean for you only to love your next-door neighbor (although you should be doing that), but your neighbors are simply those you see most frequently; those closest to you; those whom you come in contact with day by day.

You're helping yourself (and others) become free, so you can forget about yourself and be about your Father's business. Jesus was so whole He could do this. ". . . Did you not know that I must be about My Father's business?" He said (Luke 2:49).

You will be helping others in all these areas. You will be helping people listen to the Holy Spirit as He speaks Jesus' words to their spirits. They will gain God's perspective in their problem areas.

They will learn to love and forgive, as you gently guide them in this direction.

Perhaps you are saying, "I need help for myself. I'm not ready to pray for others." *Read on!* Some of the best soul-healing prayer-counselors needed prayer assistance for themselves before being ready to help other people. If you feel this way, keep the helping of others as your goal while getting help for yourself. If your own troubles are not too heavy, you may be able to begin praying with others, even while you are receiving prayer help for yourself. In any case, this book is going to help you.

Are you ready to embark on this adventure? If you are, you will be thrice blessed, because you will be carrying on one of Jesus' major ministries on earth.

Bon Voyage.

> For I looked, and there was no man; I
> looked among them, but there was no
> counselor, Who when I asked of them,
> could answer a word.
>
> Isaiah 41:28

3
Have You Heard the Call?

At our seminars we could pray with people for soul healing *en masse,* and we do that too, but when we train others to share in soul-healing prayer, we find that the work of inner healing continues long after the seminar is over. Realizing they now have a group of newly trained people, the sponsoring church or group will often feel called to continue the ministry of soul healing, making it available not only to their own people, but also to others, churched and unchurched.

We remind the people who participate in prayer-counseling at our seminars that those four days of meetings with "in-service training" of actually praying with people doesn't make them fully equipped but is a good *beginning.* We encourage them to study, pray, and grow in their knowledge and skill, while remaining under the leadership of their pastor and participating in the church family. (More details on this later on.)

People have found it very helpful to attend a "Healing of the Whole Person Seminar," but obviously not everyone can, and there are certainly other ways to learn about inner healing. All that we share in the seminars—and a great deal more—is contained in my first book on inner healing, *Emotionally Free.* "It gives clear instruction without having to go to a clinic or days of training to get started praying," says Joan Tench, Episcopal minister's wife. It's a good foundational beginning.

Reading this present book, *How to Pray for Inner Healing,* is like coming to the four-hour counselor-training session preceding our seminar, except for the class interaction, prayer demonstrations, and team experience. To compensate for these, I have given far more aids than I could give in the training session, or in the seminar itself for that matter. Most especially in-depth guidance is offered for those who want to go beyond helping pray at a seminar and ac- tually want to get involved in a ministry.

Some Encouraging Quotes

There aren't enough professional people available to meet more than a fraction of the emotional needs of the world. And even if there were, most people could not afford the expense for such help. In the light of this, let's see what trained counselors and pastors, as well as psychologists and psychiatrists, have to say about encourag- ing people to prepare themselves to help others.

The Rev. Francis MacNutt, well-known teacher and author of many fine books says in *Healing,* "The ideal, then, is that people qualified, by a gift of the Spirit, coupled with a knowledge of psy- chology, or with a great sensitivity, be available for persons who wish to pray for inner healing."

Dr. Cecil Osborne in his book *Release From Fear and Anxiety* has a most surprising thing to say about nonprofessional people helping others. He says:

Dr. Werner Mendel, professor of psychiatry at the University of Southern California, set up a three-part experiment. One group of patients was led by trained psychiatrists and the other top staff mem- bers at the hospital. A second group was led by a less adequately trained crew of psychotherapists and clinical psychologists. The third group was ministered to by persons having no formal training in therapy. *The groups led by the untrained individuals fared best.* Those treated by the most highly trained staff members showed the least improvement. Mendel was so surprised by the results that he repeated the experiment with different patients and other leaders. The results were the same. *The nonprofessional leaders did the best. . . .*

At a large mental institution on the West Coast one of the psy- chiatrists told me that they had seventy-six groups meeting several times a week. They did not have sufficient trained personnel and called upon office workers and other untrained personnel to convene the meetings. There was one group without a leader, and a staff member suggested that the truck driver be asked to lead it. "At least he can convene the group and ask them what they want to talk about," someone suggested. The staff watched Joe, the truck driver, rather carefully. At first it was to make sure that he would make no serious mistakes. Later, I was told, he was not just watched but studied because a larger percentage of his group was dismissed from the institution than from any other group; and a smaller number of his released patients returned to the hospital than from other groups. "We studied him to see how he did it," I was told.

"What did you find out?" I asked.

"Well, we discovered three things. First, he loved those people and cared about them. They sensed it, and it made a big difference. Second, he was strong and took no foolishness from them. Third, he had a native common sense and some basic insight into human nature. These three things outweighed all of the formal psychiatric training the rest of us had received." (This would indicate that the presence of love is more important than technical skills. Ideally, professional counselors should have both.)

Cecil Osborne, *Release From Fear and Anxiety,* copyright © 1976, Key-Word edition, pp. 175, 176; used by permission of WORD BOOKS, PUBLISHER, Waco, Texas 76796.

I'm not suggesting that just anyone can qualify to be a prayer-counselor, and later we will examine some of the requirements, but isn't it strange that we should be hesitant to accept the fact that many ordinary people can learn to help others, when in most churches in America relatively untrained persons are allowed to lead young people's groups and teach Bible-school classes? To these individuals we entrust the spiritual well-being of millions of children, young people, and adults with little thought—in comparison.

Characteristics of a Soul-Healing Prayer-Counselor

You don't have to be perfect in order to be involved in this work! Isn't that nice? If that were the criterion, Jesus would have had no one to follow in His footsteps. But if you can forget about yourself for a few hours while you give your full attention to someone else's needs, you can begin training to be a prayer-counselor. It's encouraging to know, too, that genuinely wanting to serve others is a mark of one who is growing in maturity.

These words came to my mind at a retreat. I don't know if I had heard them somewhere or whether they were given to me directly from the Holy Spirit, but they are certainly true.

You can only bare the sharpest pain,
in the presence of the deepest love.

1. As the counselee shares his or her pain, *the first need for you, as a minister of soul healing, is to express unconditional love.* You can do this only when you are an open channel to God's love, since human love alone is limited. Deep love makes it easier to talk about deep pain. Ask God to baptize you with His love for the person in need. God's compassion will flow through you if you are willing and open.

2. The *prayer-counselor must not be a judgmental person.* If you judge the one you are praying with in words (or even in body language), it will stop him from being open to share. People I didn't think I could love, have become lovable to me, as I learned about their backgrounds and saw the reasons why they did the things they did. This doesn't mean I excused or condoned those actions, but that as I understood them better, I was able to become a better channel of God's love and healing. You will cure the wrong behavior more effectively by loving and praying, rather than by telling the person how wrong he is.

3. *The third characteristic for a prayer-counselor is that you are able to keep confidences.* Some people can't, but the prayer-counselor *must.* Things told in prayer-counseling are *absolutely* confidential. This means you must *never,* under *any* circumstances reveal what has been told you to *any*one: not to a close friend, nor even to your husband or wife, unless the counselee has given you permission. And then be careful that you pray about it only in private, *not* at a prayer meeting—not even anonymously. You may, however, pray about the person's needs with your inner-healing prayer partner who has already been involved. You shouldn't even tell others *whom* you've been praying with without his or her knowledge and permission. Betraying confidence can hurt the very person you've been spending hours trying to help. It can damage your ministry, and that of your church. People will not come for help if they catch the least rumor that tales are being told "out of school." If you can't keep confidences, don't get into prayer-counseling.

4. *To be an effective prayer-counselor you must be a patient person, willing to wait for the Lord to give direction, and you must be patient*

with the counselee, too. Sometimes it takes people a while to get started, saying or sharing the things they need to.

5. *You must be one who knows how to listen to the Lord.* Praying for another is a good way to grow in your awareness of that inner knowing when God has spoken, and to help the person in need learn to listen also. You and your prayer partner, being Christians of some experience, will have a knowledge of Scripture and a personal walk with our Lord, so you will be able to guide the person to know when he or she has heard from Him.

6. *You must learn the art of listening with full interest and attention, so you will be sure you understand what is being said during counseling, and can, if necessary, repeat what you have heard.* You will sometimes need to be a sounding board, so the person can hear his own thoughts repeated. This can bring revelation to him. When people know you're trying to let God's unconditional love come through you, they will be willing to share with you thoughts that they've perhaps never told another person. And they may be subjects you have never heard before! You must be able to listen quietly without reacting emotionally to what you hear. Don't appear shocked about anything that is said. Listen, too, with spiritual ears, for what he says with his mouth may be different from what he really feels.

Along with this, keep eye contact with the person while he's talking, to demonstrate your concern and love. You need to be watching his facial expressions and how he's responding. Your interest will help him express his needs. If you've had a similar experience to his, you may want to interrupt and tell your story, but resist the inclination. You may share later at a more appropriate moment—but not in the middle of his counseling time. Help him receive his primary insight from God directly, not at second hand.

7. *You must be courteous.* Don't keep looking at your watch while your counselee is sharing. Try not to interrupt in the middle of a sentence. If he's gone on over the time allotted, stand up when there's a break, and reach out your hands to invite a closing prayer circle, but don't, as one counselee reported happening, stand at the door with your hand on the knob to show the time is over! You should have made the time schedule clear to the counselee at the beginning. He or she is placing great trust in you and will be highly sensitive to your attitude.

A part of courtesy is *being on time.* If you are habitually late, the counselee will get the idea you don't really think he or she is important. Let your counselee or partner know if you are going to be late. With two prayer-counselors, one can usually cover for the other, but be courteous to your prayer partner, too, and don't take advantage.

8. *You must be a positive person.* You must always give the person you're praying with hope, helping him realize that no matter how big his problem, God is bigger.

9. *You must be teachable, not having a "know it all" attitude, but desiring to continue to grow in Christ and in the ministry of soul-healing prayer.*

10. *The most important characteristic of the prayer-counselor is that you truly feel called of God to the work.* This will be confirmed to you as your prayer ministry bears fruit. Lives will be changed, relationships healed, sometimes bodies will be healed, and you will be filled with the awe of God's goodness and with His joy. On this journey in prayer you will follow in Jesus' steps to help the bruised and the brokenhearted.

Ordinary counseling can be an exhausting business. However, you will usually find that in this kind of soul-healing prayer-counseling you will feel *refreshed* afterward. This is because you will not have been carrying the burden of the counselee's troubles and problems, but showing him or her how to let Jesus lift those burdens and take them away. You will have been looking at Jesus, listening to Jesus, learning more about Jesus' love, and experiencing the joy of healing right along with the counselee. The counselors don't leave the session with the original unhappy memories any more than the counselee does—all of them leave with *healed* memories.

Prayer-Counselor Basic Requirements

I have listed some of the characteristics needed to be the kind of person to work in prayer-counseling. Now let's look at a few other requirements. No one is perfect, but you should be working to let God's life change you in these areas to be more like Jesus.

1. *You must have a personal commitment to Jesus as Lord of your life, preferably extending over several years.*

The only place the Bible says a person should not be a novice (meaning a beginner) is when seeking the advanced position of a Bishop in the Church (1 Timothy 3:6). Yet to help people with deep problems, a Christian counselor needs *stability* as well as *ability,* and this comes with experience. A new Christian could begin praying for himself and his children, even though not yet ready to reach out in a prayer ministry outside the home.

2. *You must be a praying person.* You should believe in the power of prayer, and practice it each day in your own life.

3. *You must have good general knowledge of the Bible, read it regularly, and be able to work from it.* Someone said, the Bible is our road map, and needs to be read and referred to every day to keep us on course. Any counsel or direction in prayer that you give must be in agreement with Scripture.

4. *You must be part of a church family and submitted to a pastor's godly counsel.*

5. *Your morals must be in line with the New Testament.*

6. *You must be emotionally stable, not in* serious *need of counseling yourself.*

7. *Your life should be a good example.* In so far as possible, your household should be in order, your children well managed, and your marriage given prime time. You should be clearly aware that God comes first, family second, and other responsibilities follow. There are too many people who spend all their extra time helping others, while their own lives and homes are a mess.

8. *To the best of your ability, you must have forgiven everyone, or be in the process of doing so.*

9. *You must understand the essentials of the Christian faith. You need to have grasped the meaning of the threefold nature of man.* (Again I recommend reading our book *Trinity of Man.*)

10. *You must believe God is good and wants good things for His children.* You need to be able to back this up with Scripture and personal examples. (*Moving Right Along in the Spirit,* by Dennis Bennett, chapters 1 and 2, is recommended reading.)

11. *You need to have received the Baptism or empowerment with the Holy Spirit or be presently praying about it* (Luke 24:49; Acts 1:4, 5, 8). You can't expect to be fully effective in prayer-counseling without it. Fortunately, it is as simple to receive the Baptism in the Holy Spirit as it is to receive salvation. In nearly every community today, there are churches and prayer groups where you can receive prayer help if you need it.

12. *You need to believe in and be open to receive the supernatural gifts listed in 1 Corinthians 12:7–11.* These gifts are all-important when ministering to others in soul-healing prayer.

13. *You should know how to lead a person to Jesus.*

14. *You should know how to pray with people to renounce and be delivered from the influence of cults and occult practices.*

15. *You should know how to pray with someone to receive the power of the Holy Spirit.* (Our book *The Holy Spirit and You* is recommended reading for these last five areas.)

16. *It's highly recommended that you experience soul-healing prayer yourself.* It will help you, perhaps more than you guess. You will be more able to love the person you are working with, when you are healed enough to have a healthy love for yourself. Also, it will be good to experience how it feels to be on the receiving end of prayer-counseling.

As the prayer-counselor does this work, he or she may gain insight into personal needs; also watching another person get healed raises your own confidence in the reality of the healing, and so increases your level of faith to receive healing yourself.

Two Main Ways to Pray

Ways of praying are as unlimited as the creativity of God Himself, and His ways are "past finding out" (Romans 11:33). I suppose that means we'll always be finding new ways to pray. The two I've found most helpful and recommend to you are:

1. **Reliving the Scene With Jesus**

2. **The Creative Prayer**

These forms of prayer are explained in detail in *Emotionally Free* (chapter 6), but I will review them here with further practical advice:

1. Reliving the Scene With Jesus

Let the Holy Spirit bring to the person's mind a memory that needs to be prayed about. It may be something big or something seemingly very small. It may be recent, or a long time ago. (Please refer to the next chapter, for a number of suggestions on how to help the person recall things that need to be prayed about.)

There are two phases to Reliving the Scene With Jesus. First, *ask your counselee to describe the hurtful event as clearly as possible.* Talk with him about it. Ask how it made him feel. It's important to get emotions out in the open. Allow the person to feel free to cry if he or she needs to. (Here's where a box of tissues comes in handy!) Don't feel embarrassed at this point.

Before you pray about a hurtful scene, encourage the counselee to describe any details he feels comfortable sharing. He may describe what the room looked like, what he was wearing, where he was sitting, and so forth. Everything doesn't have to be expressed in order to be healed. What you're trying to do is help the person enter into the memory. Allow him to express his feelings.

The enemy often tempts us to deny emotions such as anger, anxiety, or fear because we're not *supposed* to have them. When we see our hurts honestly for what they are, deeper healing can take place. Scripture says, " 'Be angry, and do not sin': do not let the sun go down on your wrath, nor give place to the devil" (Ephesians 4:26, 27). That means release it in an acceptable way as soon as you can. Getting in touch with our feelings, and *then praying,* is the best way to handle anger and often reveals the *cause* of those feelings. When feelings get out into the open, they can be healed, no longer being repressed, and therefore no longer controlling us. The emotion of anger isn't a sin, but holding on to it, nursing it, and injuring others with it *is.*

One man told me that just as he was getting a real release from some pent-up and previously unknown feelings, the counselor, unnerved by seeing a man cry, tried to comfort him with something like, "There, there, everything's okay; you don't need to cry about it!" He said, "That blocked me from getting the release I needed."

Of course, if the person cries uncontrollably for ten or fifteen minutes without any apparent benefit, you might well begin to put some brakes on. You can do this by drawing attention to the present surroundings and comforting thoughts. Perhaps the subject matter being talked about is too difficult for now, and you need to begin with something easier.

In addition to crying, other emotional responses may be a trembling voice, mouth or limbs, loud talking, yawning, perspiring or cold hands, laughing, and so forth. These are ways human beings release tension. The most common emotional expression during inner healing is tears of release and tears of joy.

The second step or phase in Reliving the Scene With Jesus is to *begin praying, and as you do, ask the counselee to try to see Jesus in the picture.* Remind him that Jesus was there all the time. Say to him, "When you visualize the event now, it won't hurt as it did before, because Jesus is there to heal and comfort you."

People often need some measure of inner healing before they can visualize the Lord. Tell your counselee not to worry about that. If he is not able to visualize Jesus at first, suggest that he try to *feel* Jesus' presence. If he can't do that, have him describe in words what he *thinks* Jesus would be doing and saying if he could visualize Him. Guide the prayer by asking what he is experiencing; ask what he sees (or feels) Jesus doing or hears Him saying (or what he thinks He should be doing or saying). He may want to ask Jesus some questions about the situation. Don't make other comments unless you feel what you have to say is inspired by the Holy Spirit. Always give the counselee opportunity to hear for himself first. However, words or pictures given you by the Spirit can bring guidance and a real spiritual breakthrough.

Allow plenty of time for the person to enjoy the healing presence of Jesus and to have release of his or her feelings. You may ask questions to draw the person out and guide him.

"Where do you see or feel Jesus in the scene? What is He doing? Is He close to you? If not, why not? Can you go to Him? Is Jesus speaking to you?" Encourage the person to tell Jesus what he or she is seeing and feeling.

Some people see the scene they are visualizing as if they were viewing it from outside; others can feel themselves right in the action. It works either way!

Here's a typical example of a Reliving the Scene With Jesus Prayer, one based on an actual case.

A Christian woman who had fallen away from church fellowship for some years was having many serious problems. When she heard of soul-healing prayer, it gave her new hope as her background was full of unhappy memories.

One hurtful memory she shared was that her parents told her repeatedly that she wasn't loving, and punished her for it. To try to correct this "defect" in her personality, several times a week they would make her sit in a corner, and from time to time she was supposed to show love to her brother by hugging him. At the same time, her little brother would pinch her and make faces at her when the parent wasn't looking. When told about this, the parent wouldn't believe it.

She says, "You might like to know that as a child I was always unhappy, bitter, and didn't smile or like anything going on in my world. I didn't want anybody to touch me. I always backed away, and I think a lot of this attitude was from being forced to hug, touch, and kiss in order to learn to be a loving person. All it did for me was to cause me to hate more and draw away from people more."

When prayed for, it was hard for the young woman to visualize Jesus. So her counselor said, "Just tell me what you think Jesus would do."

She said, "Well, I think He'd pick me up out of the chair and hug me. He wouldn't say anything. That's all I want anyway, someone to care and understand ... someone to love me." Having begun with merely an act yielding her will to God, she was then able to begin to feel the love of Jesus back in her childhood.

After allowing her to enjoy the comfort of Jesus' love for a while, the counselor asked if she would now forgive her parents and brother. She said, "I have done this many times." "That's good," the counselor said, "but your child-self needs to forgive from the time of the hurt." She had never thought it possible to do that. She was then led in a prayer of forgiveness, being encouraged to see herself as that child, and to forgive in that time frame.

"Through Jesus, I forgive you, Mom, Dad, and little brother. I will no longer hold this hurtful memory against you. [To her parents] You did the best you knew how to try to raise me. I set you free, and I set myself free. Jesus has healed me."

In this suggested prayer, *I will no longer hold this against you* means, *I will no longer judge you.* Scripture says, "Judge not, that you be not judged" (Matthew 7:1). All hurts in life weren't healed instantly in this young woman's life, but this one was, and she affirmed that in her prayer, "Jesus has healed me."

Before beginning to pray, she relived the memory by sharing it with the counselor, who drew her out and was supportive to her. *Through prayer,* she relived it with Jesus, released her pain and in place of it, received His healing love. And finally, she forgave from the past scene. (She had already forgiven from the present with her will, otherwise this prayer and the results would have been blocked.) These will often be the steps for this kind of prayer. (This will be explained later.)

Mary Helen Post, a dear friend, an accomplished musician, prayed by herself, reliving a scene with Jesus. It's good to be aware that a person can pray for healing by his or herself.

> God showed me a hurt I had as a child, age six or seven. My parents and brothers were in the car waiting outside the grocery, and I had been sent in for a loaf of bread. The grocer looked at me and said, "Tell your parents I will have to have some money." And that's all I let him say. I just ran back out, without the bread, and I was angry with everybody, and very frightened.
> In the reconstruction scene with Jesus, He went behind the counter and put His arm around the grocer and told him, "Don't be afraid; we'll get through this all right." Then I, *as a child,* spoke to the grocer and said "It's all right. I understand how you feel." And I wasn't angry with the folks anymore.
> This healing has a great bearing on my attitude now toward the frightening economics we're facing. But most of all I think it has just made me more *aware* of Jesus in my child heart.

With Mary Helen, forgiveness from her inner child was automatic because of Jesus' acknowledged presence with her.

Dr. Wilder Penfield, widely acclaimed neurosurgeon, did some revealing experiments which led him to the conclusion that memories and feelings are recorded together in the brain. As we recall a hurtful scene, we not only remember the facts and circumstances, but also our feelings about them. One of the values of Reliving the Scene With Jesus Prayer is that repressed feelings can be offered to God for healing.

As your counselee relives the scene with Jesus, the Lord will heal the way he or she *felt* about what happened. God Himself can't change the facts and circumstances of the past event (He doesn't contradict Himself), but He can and does heal the feelings about it, the emotions, and gives a corrected interpretation. For example, if the person's parents were divorced, that obviously can't be changed, but God can heal the hurts involved, comfort him, help him to forgive, and give him understanding about the situation.

I show in *Emotionally Free* how the risen Jesus used this kind of prayer to heal and reinstate the apostle Peter, who had denied Him before the Crucifixion. Romans 12:2 tells us to, ". . . be transformed [changed] by the renewing of your mind. . . ." This is one way our minds can be renewed. Jesus heals the hurt, as we see Him present in the scene.

> Reliving the Scene With Jesus
> is far different from
> reliving the scene without Him.

Tell your counselee that in prayer he doesn't have to relive every detail that happened in the hurtful memory. It may not be necessary to go through the whole event. Jesus is the Healer, who will lead him into the scene at the right moment. Tell him or her to relive the scene *only* from when he or she can see Jesus, sense His presence, or allow His presence to be there.

During prayer, God isn't going to blank out the old memory. "If that were the case," says the Rev. Ted Dobson in *How to Pray for Spiritual Growth,* ". . . we would not know who we are, for much of our identity comes from our previous experiences." We learn from past experiences and some of those early times did have benefits. It's as if God had a camera with which He takes a new and healed picture of an old memory and presents it to us. The old memory is there, but the new one is much stronger.

Some actions I've seen Jesus take for people in Reliving the Scene prayer are:

Step in and take a beating for a child, or for an adult; pick up a child and love it; wash a child in a sparkling stream from the effects of molestation and/or incest; explain the facts of life to a youngster; reconcile families; give insights into own and others' behavior; heal a broken heart from divorce; give loving discipline; comfort at a hospital scene; walk a child to school; help a teen on his first date, and so forth.

Visualize Happy Scenes, Too. You may ease the pressure of recalling hurtful memories by encouraging the person you are praying with to also visualize happy times in the past, realizing Jesus' presence in them. This establishes those good memories more deeply.

2. Creative Prayer

Creative Prayer is allowing God to do something new in memory and emotions. Here you have the counselee visualize scenes of things God would like to have done, or to do. The Holy Spirit will guide him in this, and profound effects can follow. "God," says the Scripture, ". . . calls those things which do not exist as though they did" (Romans 4:17). This kind of prayer allows God's creative power to help the person see what He wanted for him in the past, and wants for him now, and in the future.

Examples of This Kind of Praying. A young husband and father, Jay, says this of a Creative Prayer he was given at a seminar at Cornerstone Christian Community in Lynnwood, Washington:

> I saw myself at my favorite park, where I used to play baseball as a boy. I was at my position at second base, and my father was in the dugout, coaching as he did in Little League. Next to him was the Lord, and they were both coaching and encouraging me. It was really good.
>
> Later on the Lord took me aside and reminded me that often I did not follow my father's counsel, and that I have not followed my heavenly Father's counsel as I should. He told me that both He and my father love me.
>
> He invited me to go fishing with Him and said, "I will be a Father to you and you can be My son." I feel He wants me to tell my father how much I appreciate the interest he has taken in me especially in my youth.

A young woman named Joann had this experience with the Lord.

> As a child, I was not wanted, and all my sisters and cousins (who lived with us) would taunt me and do sadistic things to me. I would go into the woods to escape from them.
>
> I pictured myself in the woods as a child of about seven years old. I saw the Lord. He came and sat down with me there. He told me He would be my Friend, and He had come to play with me.
>
> Every game we played together I won! He told me I would always

be a winner with Him. He then lifted me up into the highest tree, and with His help, I was able to climb higher than ever before.

I had always felt as if I were a failure and that I could do nothing right. But with God—I know I am a winner! Praise His name.

Some things I've known Jesus to do in Creative Prayer are: play ball with a little boy; smile as a little girl served him lunch on a board across two logs; give a child a piggyback ride; teach a child geography; push a child in a swing; take a walk in the woods or a garden; color, swim, skate, walk on stilts; play the piano with child on his lap; climb a tree to a tree house; lie on His back watching the clouds; sit under a willow tree with a child and his dog.

What does Creative Prayer do? (Read 1 Corinthians 1:28.) It allows God to build into the person's life what he needed but missed, especially in childhood. It fills the gaps in his life with Jesus' all sufficient love, and helps him grow in his love for Him. It helps to restore his or her God-given creativity. It helps the knowledge of God move from the head to the heart. You will be amazed at how the Holy Spirit will take over and guide, when the person begins to pray this way.

If needed, you can help your counselee pray creatively for the future (or a future event). Here is an example from my own experience:

Meg met with me and my dear friend, Jeannie Lambert, to pray. (This is the same "Meg" I told about in *Emotionally Free,* chapter 1.) She was concerned about how she could survive the summer with a house full of people. She loved her extended family, but the house was too crowded with extra bodies and extra furniture. (Meg's son and grandchildren had moved in when his wife had divorced him.)

We invited Meg to visualize what a typical day might be like next summer, and live through it with Jesus. As she began her day, instead of leaving the house immediately as she normally would have done, she saw her husband still in bed and herself sitting down beside him to talk for a while. Jesus was there, too, sitting on the cedar chest.

Next she saw her grandchildren, ages six and eight. They usually allowed her to hug them but never seemed to respond. "They don't seem to need me," she noted. As she visualized them with Jesus there, Meg could see the children were hurt, and that's why they didn't respond. Jeannie suggested Meg see herself sit down on the floor and hug them—which she did.

Continuing her visualization of the future, she saw her son, sitting in the living room after coming home from work. He's overweight, and because of this, Meg doesn't like to hug him. When she tries to affirm him, he puts his head down with embarrassment, so she stops. Again, with Jesus present, she realized the reason for this was because of his hurts in his earlier days and in his present divorce. I suggested she write her affirmations in a love note to her son because it might be easier for both of them that way.

Meg remembered her father's chiding her for being overweight by saying she'd probably be like a three-hundred-pound woman they knew. Actually it was Meg's mother who was overweight; Meg never was. Meg then forgave her father and broke the power of passing on his judgment to her son. She could then feel more comfortable with the idea of hugging her son.

Meg saw Jesus with her at the end of the day there in the family room. He had His arm around her shoulder and looked pleased with her. Meg didn't feel depleted of energy as she usually would have been, just pleasantly tired.

Jeannie said, "Meg, I feel Jesus just said to you, 'Well done, my good and faithful one.'" Meg answered, "Oh, I can't receive that because it wasn't in my strength but His."

I said, "Yes, but if you don't receive this trophy, you won't have it to give back to Jesus at the end of the day."

"Okay," she said, "I'll receive it, since I can then have the joy of giving it back."

The result of this Creative Prayer for the future was that the grandchildren became more open, and everyone seemed to respond differently to Meg. Meg was changed, too, and realized that she was responding differently to them. Summer was a whole lot different because she let Jesus be Lord of it.

Note that I'm not proposing Meg was able either to foresee or change future events by this visualization, but it certainly changed her *feelings,* and consequently the response of those around her too. She allowed Jesus to be Lord of her future before she got there.

These two kinds of prayer will be the basis of what I share with you further. The Holy Spirit gives a lot of variations to this theme.

Sometimes these two kinds of prayer mesh together. In the next chapter I have listed a number of things you may pray about, together with suggested prayer patterns. I think you will find them helpful.

The Prayer of Saint Francis for You

The prayer of Saint Francis of Assisi is a good one for all who are willing to pray and counsel others. As you read, make it your personal prayer, and listen for the call from the Captain of your soul, asking you to become more and more an instrument of His healing love.

> Lord, make me an instrument of Thy peace.
> Where there is hatred, let me sow love:
> where there is injury, pardon;
> where there is doubt, faith;
> where there is despair, hope;
> where there is darkness, light;
> and where there is sadness, joy.
>
> O divine Master, grant that I
> may not so much seek to be consoled, as to console;
> to be understood, as to understand;
> to be loved, as to love;
> for it is in giving, that we receive;
> it is in pardoning, that we are pardoned;
> and it is in dying,
> that we are born to eternal life.

Do you hear the call?

... counselors of peace have joy.

Proverbs 12:20

... in a multitude of counselors there is safety.

Proverbs 24:6 KJV

4
His Presence for Your Journey

What joy and illumination to take a Scripture and try to put it into your own words. Have you ever done this? I'll give you my paraphrase of a passage which, in itself, has brought inner healing to many. It's Psalms 139:1–10; 13–18:

O Lord, You have searched my heart and known it. You know when I sit down; You know when I stand up. You understand my deepest thoughts. You carefully watch over my pathway and are with me when I lie down to rest. You know everything about me. You know everything I have to say. You walk behind me and go before me and have laid Your hand upon me. Your knowledge of me is beyond understanding.

Where could I go from Your Spirit? Or where could I go from Your presence? If I move upward to heaven, You are there. If I lie down in (my own private) hell, You are there. If I take a flight high in the sky, or if I go diving in the depths of the sea, Your hand shall lead me, and Your right hand will hold me.

You fashioned my inmost being from the start. Your presence covered me in my mother's womb. I praise You for I am wonderfully and intricately made. Even when I was being formed, my inner parts and bones taking shape before birth, You watched over me. You knew my every movement and knew me long before I was born and took my first breath. My life was recorded in Your book.

O God, Your thoughts of me are so precious and so many, they're like the grains of sand in the sea—unable to be numbered. When I awake each morning, You are still with me.

God is always present with us. We need to acknowledge this, live it, and help others do so. God was there at the time of your conception and birth, and through your life right up to the present. He goes with you through the day and wants to guide your pathway. He is with you every moment. Even when you choose to ignore Him, though He's not happy about it, He still goes with you. He's with you when you go to bed at night, and is there when you wake up in the morning. His hands are holding you. He will be with you to the end of your time on earth, and if you accept Him, He will be with you in heaven.

Master Keys

Here are two master keys for you to use, as you help people in prayer-counseling.

Key 1. **That God loves us unconditionally**

Key 2. **That He is with us in every moment of our lives**

If God weren't love, the news that He is always present would not be good news; but because He loves us *unconditionally,* we can fearlessly see Him present with us in everything. However, you need to realize—and point out to the people you will be counseling—that even though He was there, God wasn't approving of the bad things that may have been happening. His presence and power weren't known or acknowledged at the time, however, and since He has given us freedom, He will only change things in our lives as we permit Him to. (*See* Matthew 13:58.) Now He is ready and willing to heal those past hurts, as you pray together.

If the person you pray with isn't sure of God's unconditional love and His omnipresence, show them to him in the Scripture. Chapter 5 in *Emotionally Free* will assist you. But even though the Scriptures don't convince him, the Lord will reach him and show him as you pray together. (For further reading on the sovereignty of God see Dennis Bennett's *Moving Right Along in the Spirit,* chapters 1 and 2.)

Why a Prayer Partner?

I think it's best to pray with a partner, since that's the way the Lord led me at the beginning of my ministry in this field—and I've seen the wisdom in doing so more and more. Our Lord set the pattern of "two by two." Luke reports, ". . . the Lord . . . sent them two by two before His face into every city and place where He Himself was about to go" (Luke 10:1). We go before Him two by two and prepare the way for His healing ministry in this present day.

My husband and I have traveled and ministered in hundreds of churches since we were married in 1966, and now and then we hear of a minister or counselor who has become emotionally involved with a counselee. Sometimes, as a result, homes are broken, and an excellent ministry is detoured or stopped altogether. If the person had only made it a rule to work with a partner in counseling, the tragedy could have been averted. It takes some planning to get two capable counselors together, but the effort is worth it.

The prayer-partner relationship itself can be a problem. Dennis's mother used to say, "There is no such thing as a platonic relationship!" Wherever a man and a woman work closely together, there is always the possibility of a romantic attachment forming. There is real value in having teams made up of a man and a woman, but I recommend strongly that they be husband and wife. In this combination, there is both the masculine and the feminine understanding of the counselee, *but closeness between the partners is not a problem but a blessing.* Outside of husband and wife teams, it's usually best for two women to work together, or two men. Two women can safely pray for a woman, and under certain circumstances, for a man. Two men should not normally pray for a woman alone. Then too, sometimes a counselee doesn't want to have a member of the opposite sex there during prayer-counseling. A general rule is that at least one member of the team should be the same sex as the person with whom they're praying.

Other Reasons for Praying in Twos

1. *It gives the counselee twice the resources.*
2. *The counselors can help one another and learn from one another in a team.* If one comes to an impasse, the other can step in. "Two

are better than one, Because they have a good reward for their labor. For if they fall, one will lift up his companion . . ." (Ecclesiastes 4:9, 10).

3. Although God is everywhere, and He dwells within believing people, Jesus teaches that *"where two or three" are together He will be with them in a special way.* He also says, ". . . if two of you agree on earth concerning anything that they ask, it will be done for them by My Father in heaven" (Matthew 18:19).

4. *It gives the Holy Spirit more opportunity to minister His gifts.* "For to one is given the word of wisdom through the Spirit, to another the word of knowledge through the same Spirit" (1 Corinthians 12:8). It's a good way for prayer-counselors to grow in the gifts of the Spirit.

5. *The counselee doesn't get too dependent on one person (transference).* Instead, if handled properly, the counselee transfers his dependence to Jesus.

6. *Shared ministry is lighter.* Prevents burnout.

7. *It helps to talk prayer needs over, but since everything shared in a prayer-counseling session is in strictest confidence, a lone counselor has no one to talk and pray with.* However, the prayer partners can freely talk and pray with one another without breaking confidentiality.

8. *If one prayer partner is away for an extended trip, or moves away, the other prayer-counselor will be there to maintain continuity when a replacement is chosen.*

9. *Sometimes a counselee will call a prayer-counselor, wanting to discuss problems at length.* The counselor can tactfully correct this by saying he does not want to discuss things without all three being present, as he doesn't want to get ahead of the other partner.

10. *There is always another witness to what takes place.* This is protection (Matthew 18:16).

11. *It's always wise to have another person present in case deliverance prayer is used* (Leviticus 26:8; Deuteronomy 32:30).

12. *It's important for an experienced prayer-counselor to occasionally have a beginner as a partner; in this way another person gets experience and the ministry grows.* Working in twos and training this way is the secret of those churches that have a growing prayer-counselor ministry.

How to Work With a Prayer Partner

When prayer-counselors work together, they must be careful there is no competition between them for the counselee's approval or attention. They should try not to draw the counselee to themselves but rather to Jesus. Self-centeredness must go to the Cross. Working with a partner will from time to time bring up some of your own unhealed hurts!

It's good to try to take turns leading, so the counselee won't relate to one of you more than the other. In one session, one may have a more prominent role, and, hopefully, the next time it will reverse. Taking turns can't be forced, but if you are aware of the need to share the leadership, it will balance out. If one counselor is a more dominant type, when he can, he should defer to the other and pray silently for God to use him or her. Romans 12:10 reminds us, "Be kindly affectioned one to another with brotherly love; in honour preferring one another" (KJV). (Be sure you agree who is to take the lead in such things as closing the session when the time is up.)

If you, an experienced counselor, are training a new counselor, you will of course tend to take the lead much of the time. You can still do things such as asking the other to lead in the opening and closing prayers, and find other ways to involve him or her.

If during prayer time you have a disagreement with your prayer partner, don't reveal it to the counselee. If you're hurting about it, practice the presence of Jesus, *then* talk over the problem later and pray about it. Counselors *must* be in love and charity with one another.

Commend your prayer partner if God especially uses him or her. If you tend to put your partner down and find it hard to affirm him or her, or if you want to dominate, you may need some healing yourself for feelings of inadequacy.

[*The counseling time during a seminar is also an opportunity for teaching people to counsel. There will be a more experienced counselor who functions as a team leader, and then one—or sometimes two—apprentice counselors. Where there are two in addition to the team leader, the leader should choose one to be the active partner, and ask the other to pray silently unless he or she receives a very special revelation. Too many participants can confuse the counselee. With the next counselee, the team leader will reverse the roles, and work with the other prayer partner.*]

Before Making a Commitment to Pray

If you don't know the person who asks you to pray with him or her, before you begin, you need to ask a few basic questions to help determine whether you will commit yourself to this prayer-counseling relationship. If you are working through your church or other group, the coordinator should have asked these questions of the person before requesting you to prayer-counsel with him or her:

1. *Are you presently seeing a counselor of some kind, such as a psychiatrist, psychologist, marriage consultant or other?*

Some people like to go from counselor to counselor, or perhaps to several at a time! If the person you are asked to help is regularly seeing another counselor, he should be told you will consider working with him (or her) when the sessions with the other counselor are completed.

2. *Have you been under psychiatric care, or hospitalized due to emotional problems? Are you presently taking any kind of drugs?*

If the person has been under psychiatric care or was hospitalized, or is on some kind of medication, you will want to decide, with your pastor's or other skilled guidance, whether you should work with him.

Be cautious about getting involved with someone who is so severely damaged that he or she is suicidal, or lives much of the time in a fantasy world. Only the most experienced prayer-counselors should handle such. And, if possible, they should talk to the doctors who have treated the person before beginning ministry. This can be an opportunity, too, to build good relationships with these professionals, and give opportunity for witness.

Preparing the Counselee to Pray

Before you begin, and as you go along, encourage the person you will be praying with to read books about inner healing, or have him listen to tapes which teach about it. Encourage him to attend a seminar on the subject, if one is available. The more prepared he is, the faster you can move ahead.

Preparing Yourself, the Counselor, to Pray

Check to see that no known sin in your life is affecting your relationship with God. If there is, confess it and ask Jesus to cleanse you. Receive His forgiveness, and make sure you've forgiven everyone, to the best of your ability, even if only on the level of your will. If you're finding it hard to forgive, you may need to have someone to help you pray through the problem.

Claim the protection of the blood of Jesus (Revelation 12:11). Ask God to keep you filled with the Holy Spirit and to guide your thoughts and words. Check your armor to see if you have it all on! (Read Ephesians 6:10–18.) Teach your family how important all of this is for them. What affects them will also affect you.

Where and How Long to Meet

If you don't know the counselee, it's best to meet on neutral ground, such as the church. After you get acquainted, you may feel free to meet in a home. It is best to have the person come to your house, rather than your going to his or hers. (If the person you're to pray with is bedridden or a shut-in, you will of course need to meet in his or her home.) Pick a room that is private and quiet, with no television or radio blaring, or other distracting noises going on. Take the telephone off the hook and/or bury it somewhere in a drawer!

Some earthy questions! Is your breath okay? No onions, or garlic, or other unpleasantness? Don't forget those important letters of the alphabet: B.O. Breath sweeteners and deodorants can be a real support to ministry! Remember to have a box of tissues handy for the counselee.

An hour and a half is a good regular length for your sessions. Let your counselee know when you begin your meetings, what the time frame is, and stick to it. Don't let things drag out, or allow long periods of discussion. There will be times the person needs to talk things over before praying, but be careful the talk is not to avoid prayer.

[*At a seminar, the total time for sharing and prayer for each person is about forty minutes. Nevertheless, much can be accomplished because the groundwork has already been laid during the general teaching sessions. The amount of preparatory talk must, of course, be kept to a minimum; the majority of time should be spent in* prayer. *During the teaching sessions, the Holy Spirit has already pointed out memories which need healing. That one period of prayer isn't expected to heal an entire life, but great strides can be made in this setting. The person learns how to pray for healing, and so can continue on by him or herself or seek further prayer-counseling assistance.]*

The First Meeting

The first meeting with the counselee may take two hours, since you may need a full hour to get acquainted and build rapport before you start praying. If you don't know the person, or if he hasn't been to a "Healing of the Whole Person" seminar for preparation, you will want to ask these beginning questions to find out where he or she is spiritually.

Three Preliminary Questions. [Note: For seminar counselors, the three following questions will have been taken care of the first night of our seminar, so will not be necessary to go over again, unless the person missed the first meeting and especially the prayer session following.]

1. *Do you have a personal relationship with Jesus? Tell me about it.* If counselee hasn't accepted the Lord, and wants to do so, pray for him to receive Jesus into his life. (Suggested prayer is in Appendix 1.)

Being a Christian is a helpful step prior to soul-healing prayer but some people cannot come to Jesus until they have this prayer help first. If the person isn't ready to accept Jesus but is willing for you to pray healing prayers in His name, then go ahead. Because of negative parental relationships or other trauma, some people may be afraid of God and unwilling to come to Jesus until they receive some emotional healing. Even though your counselee may not have yet received Him as Savior, Jesus was present with him throughout his life, and would like to have helped him. As you pray, and as he realizes Jesus' love for him, he will very likely decide to accept Him. (For an example of this see *Emotionally Free*, pages 68–71.)

2. *Have you ever been involved with the cults or the occult?*

You may need to explain what is meant by a cult. It isn't easy to define a "cult," but the word usually means an exclusivist religious group which embraces beliefs that differ basically from scriptural Christianity. Most cults deny that Jesus is God incarnate and often deny the reality of human sin.

Occult practices attempt to reach out spiritually to gain power or information. The spiritual world that is contacted, however, is under the power of Satan—the so-called psychic realm. Therefore, the person is open to demonic influence. Some examples of the occult are: fortune-telling in any form (including the Ouija Board and tarot cards), mind reading, clairvoyance, contact with departed spirits, astrology, astral projection, and witchcraft.

Point out that God is ready to forgive him or her for past involvement in these things; also that they can block the flow of the Holy Spirit, interfere with inner healing, and need to be renounced before beginning prayer-counseling. A suggested form of prayer for renouncing cults and occult will be found in Appendix 2, or read chapter 4 of *The Holy Spirit and You.*

3. *Have you been baptized in the Holy Spirit? Tell me about your experience.*

If they want this empowering of the Spirit, pray yourself or make an appointment with someone who has an effective prayer ministry in this area. (Again, *The Holy Spirit and You* will help. Chapters 4 and 5 give detailed instructions. Involvement in the cults or occult *must* be renounced before prayer for this experience.)

The Baptism with the Holy Spirit is a great help to soul-healing prayer because it gives the counselee inner strength to cope with problems and also increased perception into areas of need. Though this is true, it should also be known that some people cannot be empowered with the Spirit without having inner-healing prayer first.

Here's an example of what I mean. Marie, a friend who does prayer-counseling, told me this:

> I prayed with a young woman who wanted the Baptism with the Spirit. The girl couldn't seem to respond. She looked very worried, and kept crying unhappily. "What's wrong?" I asked.
>
> "Oh," she sobbed, "I'm so unworthy, and I don't feel the joy and love you're talking about!"
>
> "I think," said I, "you're in need of inner-healing prayer," so I invited her into a group I was working with.

After I had gotten well into the subject, the young lady responded with excitement, "All of a sudden I know what the block is! Because of my father's own rigid background, he never could show us kids affection. The only warmth he gave me as a child was to pinch me! I know now that this lack of affection and warmth has carried over into my relationship with God!"

She remembered that she never could do things well enough to please her father. We prayed about some specific incidents, and let Jesus heal them. It was beautiful to see the joy and radiance flood the girl's face, and then she was ready to pray to receive the freedom of the Holy Spirit she had been longing for.

Questions and Suggestions to Locate Areas for Prayer

Here are some questions that may help you understand problem areas to pray about with the counselee, getting an "unofficial" kind of history:

"Are your parents living? Was or is their marriage happy? Are they divorced? Is there a stepparent? Foster parents? If a parent or parents are deceased, what was the cause of death? How old were you when one or both parents died? Were you adopted? Are you an only child or do you have siblings? Where did you come in the order of births? Do you feel you were wanted? What was your birth like? Describe any special or traumatic situations connected with it. Did you know your grandparents?"

You might ask the person to fill in the blank in the statement, "My father made me feel like a _____." You may have him or her do the same with mother, siblings, neighbors, others.

Another simple starter is to ask: "Why have you come for prayer?" or, "What do you want God to do for you?"

You might have the person go over the checklist on pages 54 and 55 in *Emotionally Free* and write his responses before your first meeting. This will give you some clues about where you may pray.

More Questions and Specific Directions for Soul-Healing Prayer

The following are suggestions to use and refer to in your prayer-counseling ministry. I think you'll find them helpful.

1. *Who is the first person you ever* felt *really loved you?* Have the person answer this from how he felt in his early years, *not* how he feels or understands now as an adult.

Explain that he's not being asked to blame anyone, but to pinpoint relationships which may need healing. If he didn't feel loved by either father or mother, his foundational years did not have what God intended him to experience. The great thing is that God can fill in the gap where human love was missing. This first question, when answered truthfully, has been one of the most helpful ones in giving me understanding of a person's basic needs.

Reliving the Scene Prayer. His answer will show a need for prayer, or an area for rejoicing for a good beginning. If he felt loved by one parent only, his relationship with the other parent will need to be prayed about. Have him pray about scenes with one or both parents, as God brings them to his memory.

Creative Prayer. Another way to have your counselee pray about a parent is to ask God to show him his parent as a child, thereby helping him understand why his father or mother had certain personality problems. Help him forgive them from this vantage point, since it's easier to forgive a child than an adult. Perhaps he can visualize that child-parent sitting on his knee, as he forgives him or her!

If your counselee didn't feel loved by anyone until adulthood, this indicates great deprivation and possibly longer prayer-counseling. If he has never felt loved by *any* human being, he is one of the more damaged persons whom God has rescued. If he is in either of these categories, then ask him or her question (*a*).

(*a*) "Did you live in a fantasy world in your childhood?" People who did not feel loved as children often create a fantasy world to help them survive. If the answer is affirmative, then ask him the next question.

(*b*) "Do you now, in your adult life, often escape into a fantasy world?" If the answer is *yes,* you are dealing with a most deeply hurt person who will need a longer period of prayer-counseling.

This two-part question, answered affirmatively, has in my experience, indicated a person in serious need of healing prayer. Be sure you are ready to take on such a lengthy work, perhaps as long as a year. Don't start with the person unless you intend to continue. Someone like this doesn't need any more rejection.

Creative Prayer. When he feels comfortable enough, have the person you are praying with tell about his fantasy world. He or she may never have shared it with anyone else. Talking about it will probably be a relief. It will give you some more clues for prayer. You may need to pray about this area a number of times. Some fantasizing is merely like daydreaming, and some other is clearly demonic, often with a strong sexual hook in it. If the latter is the case, review chapter 15 in *Emotionally Free*.

2. *Do you accept and love yourself when you were a child, say kindergarten through elementary school age?* (If the answer is *yes,* go on to question number 3.) If your counselee's reply is something like, "No, I can't stand that little kid," then he is not ready to pray about childhood memories. They will be too threatening for now.

Reliving the Scene Prayer. You may begin your prayer time by asking "At what age *did* you accept yourself?" and find out what hurtful memories need prayer in that time frame. You will find that as he receives healing for other hurts, he will gradually come to accept his child-self, and be ready to pray about memories of his childhood. He or she will eventually need to love and accept his or her inner child in order to be an integrated person.

3. *Were you happy as a child?* If the answer is *no* ask, "What is your first hurtful memory?" This is the question we asked Meg, remember?

Reliving the Scene Prayer. Pray about the memory that is recalled. Often as he finishes praying for one memory, another will come to mind. If several memories surface together, choose the least traumatic one to begin with; then pray about the others. If he was unhappy but doesn't understand why, the memories may be buried or situations may have been too subtle for him to understand. Prenatal prayer may be in order. I'll be telling about it in chapter 7.

4. Sometimes the person will remember little or nothing up to a certain age, say seven years old.

Reliving the Scene Prayer. If this is so, begin there, ask what the first hurtful memory was at that age, and pray about it. Often what happened at age seven may be the hurt which caused the earlier memories to be blocked, and as it is healed, earlier memories will come to mind. Do not probe the blanked-out years but trust the Holy Spirit to bring up what the person is ready to handle.

Happy memories are often covered over by the unhappy ones. As the unhappy ones are healed, the happy ones are remembered.

5. Another way to get a clue to hidden memories is to pray about a present situation. You may find it helpful to ask, "What situations have been bothering you lately? Have you had any upsets this past week?" (This is good to ask after some other clear-cut problems have already been prayed about, and you're looking for further direction.)

Reliving the Scene Prayer. After the problematic situation has been fully described ask, "Is there anything in your childhood that this reminds you of?" and then pray about it.

If the person remembers any previous good situations with a person they later experienced a trauma with, it is sometimes good to relive the good memory with him or her and Jesus, before praying about the difficult scene.

6. An interesting way to discover emotional needs is suggested by a friend and prayer-counselor, Sharon Persson. If someone has an overwhelming negative emotion, such as fear, which seems to control his life, have him write the name of that emotion in the middle of a piece of paper and circle it. Then have him draw a line like a spoke coming from the middle and write on it one kind of fear. Continue to do the same thing with all the fears that come to mind.

I've appropriated her idea in this way. Have the person write down his childhood fears. Then have him write adult fears on other spokes. (Or you may start with adult fears and go to childhood ones.) When finished, ask the person if he can see any connection between the childhood and adult fears. Discuss these connections. (Sharon also suggested doing this in a positive way. For instance take the word *peace* and write down the situations that make the person feel peaceful.)

Reliving the Scene Prayer. Pray about memories connected with the childhood emotions. As you do, you may find that the related adult fears have been healed without having to pray about them specifically, or you may feel you should go on to deal with some or all of the adult memories.

7. Sometimes a person has experienced repeated hurts in the same general area, but can't recall a specific one.

Reliving the Scene With Jesus Prayer Combined With Creative Prayer. If this is so, he may allow the Holy Spirit to create a composite scene. Let him or her visualize a typical situation where the hurt would have occurred, and pray about that. For example, one woman remembered working with her mother cleaning motel rooms. The mother was always critical, never approving. The girl visualized a typical scene in a motel room with her mother, and let Jesus deal with it, healing many memories at the same time.

8. If the counselee can't remember any specific happy scene in childhood, ask him to recall some *activity* he knows he enjoyed as a child.

Creative Prayer. Through prayer, help him accept Jesus' presence with him (flying a kite, skating, biking, drawing, coloring, playing games, and so forth). This is where God can build into his memories the love he missed. He may do things the person never experienced before. Dennis testifies to the power of this kind of prayer. Visualizing a scene of Jesus drawing pictures with him and a friend at age seven, he received a healing that he says has changed some deep root attitudes in his life (see *Emotionally Free,* pages 83–86).

9. The person may remember a time in his childhood when he felt unhappy but can't remember a scene to pray about.

Creative Prayer. Help the counselee visualize himself as clearly as possible at that time, and try to remember how he felt. Bring those feelings of fear (or whatever) to Jesus to allow Him to create a healing scene. (Sometimes looking at or remembering an old photograph can help the person visualize himself as he was.)

10. Ask the person what he or she missed and feels cheated of in his childhood or teens.

Creative Prayer. Have the counselee let Jesus be to him the Person he needed as a youth. If he needed a loving, caring schoolteacher, let him ask Jesus to let him see Him in that role; if he needed someone to help celebrate his birthday, ask Jesus to do that; if he needed someone to teach him to play some sport, let him ask Jesus to do that; if he needed someone to teach him the "facts of life," let him ask Jesus to do that! Tell him to ask Jesus to fill in the gaps of his life—to walk with him and talk with him.

11. As wounds with parents have been dealt with in Reliving the Scene Prayer, then go back and have Creative Prayer, seeing the parent as Jesus wanted him or her to be, and receive the love and affection which was originally blocked.

12. An idea for Creative Prayer

See yourself with Jesus in a scene from the Bible. You may be with Him as He heals the sick, or preaches on the hillside, or perhaps on the Emmaus Road. You may see yourself as one of the people He comes to help or to heal.

13. Creative Future Prayer

Perhaps you have a meeting coming up that you're dreading, or you don't think you can stand the last ten days of your job before vacation. Perhaps you know you're going to be entertaining a house full of people, and wonder how you're going to manage it. Do with it as Meg did earlier in this chapter. God is outside of time. By faith, visualize the future scene with Jesus and let Him be with you in the situation before it happens. When you actually get to that point, you'll find a renewed inner support and strength.

14. Reliving Scene With Jesus

You can, with Jesus, also walk through a typical day or a specific day from the past to heal some old wounds.

I've given you many suggested avenues of prayer, and there will be many additional ones in chapters 6 and 7. Some will be more meaningful to you than others, and you will most likely be given new ways of praying of your own. I learn new ways to pray through praying with others, and so will you. God is the epitome of creativity, and I repeat, "His ways are past finding out." Depend on the

Holy Spirit, and use all the helps He provides. Remember, one word from God can cut through a lot of human reasoning.

It's important for you, the prayer-counselor, to practice the presence of Jesus in your daily life, as well as during prayer with others! At your prayer sessions, acknowledge Jesus' presence within you and around you, and seek to see the person you are praying with through the eyes of Jesus.

This journey in prayer is so rewarding, especially when you see shipwrecked lives being restored and getting back on course. It's been said that happy people are those who are helping others. Of course you're not doing it for that reason, but that's just one of the bonuses.

A Prayer for Counselors

I'll close this chapter with a prayer for those who want to help others:

> Lord Jesus, it was said of You, "The Spirit of the Lord is upon me, because He has anointed Me . . ." (Isaiah 61:1–3). We want this said of us as it was of You.

> Anoint me, Lord Jesus—great Head of the Church. Pour out Your Spirit upon me! Let the anointing which is on You flow down to me as a member of Your Body, as the oil which was put on Aaron's head, when he was anointed High Priest, flowed down to his beard, and even to the hem of his garment (Psalms 133:2).

> You promised that I would be anointed with fresh oil (Psalms 92:10). Please take away any staleness in my life and fill it with Your freshness. Release me from any bondage known or unknown. Isaiah 10:27 says the anointing will break the yoke. I believe and receive these promises now.

> O mighty anointed One, cause the Holy Spirit, the Spirit of wisdom and understanding, the Spirit of counsel and might, the Spirit of knowledge and of the fear of the Lord (Isaiah 11:2), to rest on me so that I may be an effective minister to those in need.

> Dear Jesus, You were anointed with the oil of gladness beyond all others (Hebrews 1:9). Let that oil of joy anoint me also from within so that I may be continually refreshed in this calling.

> I ask all this in the name of our Lord, Jesus Christ. Amen.

(This was inspired by a prayer in *Acts/Twenty-Three* magazine.)

The counsel of the Lord stands forever,
The plans of His heart to all generations.
Psalms 33:11

5
When You Pray

Only a few of the previously suggested forms of prayer will be used in your first time of prayer, but it's good to have as much knowledge as possible for the Holy Spirit to draw from.

You have now explored the counselee's needs and possible avenues for prayer, and you're ready to begin praying. Move your chairs closer together, and if acceptable, join hands in loving support. It is a kind of laying-on-of-hands on one another, so God's Spirit can flow through your physical beings. The importance of the healing touch is known widely, and Jesus told us to do it. (Some people don't want to be touched, so abide by what makes the counselee comfortable.)

Ask the Holy Spirit Where to Begin

Remember, although you've done your homework and have a lot of information, it's still important each time to ask the Holy Spirit where to begin. Ask God to guide each one of you and request that the gifts of the Spirit, such as wisdom, knowledge, discernment, and so forth, be given as needed. Spiritual gifts may be imparted to any of you, including the counselee, and you should expect them. Be on the alert for mental pictures that can guide you, too. If any of you has a picture come to his or her mind, share it. It may be important.

When you feel the Lord has given direction, you may break hands, share it, and ask whether the others feel a confirmation. If any of you feel the Lord has given you a different direction, say so.

It's good to agree on what to pray about, and to pray about specific things rather than generalities.

[*If you're praying at a "Healing of the Whole Person" seminar, it is usually easier to know what to pray about the first time together, since there have been several hours of teaching on inner healing and also some group prayers. Fred Blanchett, a prayer-counselor and friend, described praying at a seminar like this: "It's like plucking ripe plums off a tree!" This is because only those who have a definite scene (or scenes) given by the Holy Spirit are encouraged to go for prayer-counseling ministry. If a person didn't understand my directions and doesn't clearly know why he or she has come for prayer, then you may need to use some of the questions in chapter 4 to guide you.*]

Now you have your direction, and when soul-healing prayer begins, instead of making a complete circle, prayer partners usually find it best not to join hands, making it a semicircle. Also be sure to leave one of the counselee's hands free for wiping his or her eyes; one of the prayer partners may lay a hand on a shoulder, instead of holding a hand. It's important for everyone to be comfortable; you don't want anyone to end up with a backache, or then you'll have to pray for physical healing!

Encourage the person to acknowledge Jesus' presence there with Him in the scene. He may be able to visualize Jesus; if not, encourage him to make a verbal picture of Jesus; that is to say, what he feels Jesus would do. He may want to ask Jesus some questions about the situation. Guide the prayer by asking what he is experiencing; ask what he sees (or feels) Jesus doing or hears Him saying. Don't give advice or answers unless you've given the counselee opportunity to hear for himself first, and unless what you have to say is inspired by the Holy Spirit.

Allow plenty of time for the person to enjoy the healing presence of Jesus and to have release. If you have been praying about reliving a hurtful scene (often this kind of prayer comes first), then leading him or her in a forgiveness prayer will be helpful.

Helping to Forgive

When it seems the right time, lead the counselee to speak forgiveness to those who have wronged him. Go easy at this point in your first prayer times together. Say something like this:

"You've probably tried to forgive this person. But what I'd like you to do is forgive from the past, seeing yourself and the person at the time of the incident Jesus just healed." For example:

"Through Jesus, I forgive you [name person] for [the injury]. I will no longer hold this against you [meaning, *I will not judge*]. You did the best you knew how. Because Jesus has healed me. I can forgive you freely."

Usually it's good for you to repeat this prayer and have the person follow you in it, phrase by phrase, until he gets the idea. You don't have to pray this prayer exactly, but it's the one the Holy Spirit gave me during the beginning of my ministry, so is the one I normally use.

In case the person or persons in the past event are not physically present in the room, or are no longer alive, please understand that I'm not proposing some kind of telepathy or communication with the departed, which is strictly against God's rules! The forgiveness is offered as in the past, and to the people who were alive at the time. If you prefer, you may pray this way:

"Dear Jesus, please tell [name the person] these words: 'I forgive you for [name injury]. I will no longer hold this against you. You did the best you could. Jesus is setting me free to forgive everyone. He has healed me.' "

We can't determine where a person has gone after this life, and we don't always know where he is in this world, but we can give Jesus the message and be sure He will take care of those details. He is our only mediator and advocate. If the idea of keeping our Lord busy with messages bothers you, think of the computers we have on earth and realize that if man can process data the way he does today, God is certainly big enough to handle all our prayer needs!

Praying from the scene in the past, in the first person, and the present tense seems to reach our emotions to heal them on a deep level. We are, in essence, forgiving at the time of the injury, which Jesus would have liked us to do originally. There are various reasons why we didn't. We didn't know Jesus, or were hurting too much to even think of Him. We didn't know we could appropriate Jesus' presence at the time to help us forgive on the spot. One of our goals in the present should be to learn to forgive *immediately,* so we don't need to go back and pray about it later.

Three Steps to Forgiveness

1. *The first step is to forgive from the will.* When you forgive others, God forgives you, and cleanses you by the blood of Jesus. (If you are a Christian you will probably already have done this.) If you don't take this step of yielding your will, you will block inner-healing prayer until you do. Even if it's hard, you can say, "I can't do it in my own strength, but with God's strength I choose to forgive." You may feel, "I just *can't* forgive," but can you say, "I *want* to forgive," or even, "I *want* to *want* to!" God will accept your honesty, and as you release the problem to Him, He will give you the power.

2. Some may find their needs have been met with step number one. If not, *the next step is to receive soul-healing prayer, either the creative kind or reliving the scene with Jesus.*

3. *The third step is, after Reliving the Scene With Jesus Prayer, to speak forgiveness from the age at which the hurt occurred.* (Creative Prayer may or may not use this step.) It isn't necessary to do this in order to be forgiven and cleansed by the blood of Jesus (see step 1) but it will help heal and release your emotions.

Ending the First Session

As the hour-and-a-half-allotted time comes to an end, be looking for an appropriate place to finish. Don't be abrupt about this, of course, but on the other hand, don't be hesitant to close on time. You may accomplish far more next time with rested minds than you would by going on and on this time. A good way to signal the end of the session is to stand, reach out to join hands, and begin to praise the Lord for what He has been doing.

Don't let the final moments of your time degenerate into discussing another problem or any other negative conversation. Praise the Lord, say good-bye to one another, and *go!* We often end with a "holy huddle"—a general hug, with arms around the three of us together. This kind of physical comfort is important. In mixed counseling, be careful of individual hugging; avoid "bear hugs" and anything that is too intimate. The flesh gets in so easily, and that can really spoil things.

Finally, get out your calendars and be sure you are agreed on the next time and place of meeting.

Encourage your counselee to keep a journal of what God has done each time, and you, as prayer-counselors, do the same. Information in your journal should be kept anonymously, with counselee's name in a code no one would recognize. The counselee needs to meditate on what God has done, and a good way to do this is by writing it down. As one counselor says, "Groove it into the mind!"

A Sample Page From My Journal:

Date, names of counselors, name of counselee, in code. (You could take initial of his or her last name and put it first, pick a vowel to follow, then add initial of first name.)

Bek's need today is for her will to be healed and strengthened. Wants prayer for her will to become one with God's will. We did some simple deliverance prayers for release from: false guilt, confusion, self-pity, rejection, rebellion, a counterfeit will that tries to play God. Bek followed in each prayer, then we asked God to fill the empty places with the Holy Spirit.

When asked if she felt anything special during any of these prayers, Bek said, "The deliverance prayer for the will made me realize that my mother crushed mine when I was ten years old by beating me, until I finally gave up and felt I had no more will." Looking at Bek I could see the result of this broken will in her slumped shoulders and passive manner. She went on, "My mother looked at me with such hate in her eyes, and I hated her back."

When we began to pray Bek could only see Jesus in a distant corner of the room. (Where Jesus is seen in the reconstruction prayer often gives a picture of how worthy the person feels.) "I feel, *If my mother hates me so much I must be a terrible person.*"

REQUEST Ask Jesus if this is true.
RESPONSE I can't hear Him.
REQUEST Look at Jesus' eyes. What do they say?
RESPONSE Jesus loves me.
REQUEST Then what your mother feels must be wrong?
RESPONSE That's right.

Gift of knowledge given counselor: "I see something at your feet like a limp cloth."

RESPONSE I believe that's my will—it's dead.
REQUEST Can you give it to Jesus?
RESPONSE Yes. Jesus, this is my will. I give it to You. He's got it now and He's molding it and making something good out of it. Now He's put a light in it, and He's putting it back into me. It didn't even hurt when He did that! He told me He's made it strong.

Insight given Bek. "My mother doesn't really hate me, she's just angry and frustrated." She then spoke words of forgiveness to her mother, but when through, she still saw a mental picture of her mother's angry eyes.

Bek realized she needed to ask Jesus to forgive her for hating her mother in return.

The counselor asked Jesus to put His healing hands on Bek's eyes. Bek saw her mother's eyes soften. She felt her mother say, "I don't hate you; I love you."

Root Cause: Today the Lord showed us a key to the reason Bek hasn't been strong enough to resist behavior she knows isn't right—behavior which has been the cause of destroying many friendships.

Result of Prayer: God made a breakthrough in healing her will.

Further Prayer Needed: Prayer for God's affirmation and further healing of self-identity.

Next Meeting and How to Finalize Prayer-Counseling

At subsequent meetings, take the first half-hour for sharing what's been happening, and reviewing the previous session; then pray for an hour. During this sharing time, you, your prayer partner, and the counselee should review what God revealed in the previous session. You may want to refer to one of the journals to help refresh your memory, especially if you're praying for several different people in the course of a week. Ask if the Holy Spirit has given further memories or insights to the counselee in the time between the meetings. Then go on with prayer as usual.

During the first few sessions you and your prayer partner should be able to determine how difficult the person's needs are. Occasionally a person will be dramatically helped by just one session, but most will need to meet weekly for three to six weeks. Those who are more deeply hurt may need as much as six months or more of ministry. Sometimes, due to schedules, the best you can do is meet every other week, which of course slows down the process.

If the needs are so great that the person may need to meet over a long period, and you do not feel you can do this, make other arrangements, as soon as you can, *before* you become involved. Your prayer partner may need to select another person to fill your place. Also, you may feel the seriousness of the person's problems goes beyond your ability to cope. You will then need to lovingly refer him or her on to someone with more expertise.

If a person is coming a long distance for counsel (from another state, for example) he may want to plan to come once a month and spend two consecutive days, with one or perhaps two sessions each day.

Do remember that you are there to pray for *soul healing* and *not* to give psychological counseling. If after your second or third meeting, it's evident the counselee does *not* want to pray, but rather wants only to talk over his problems, it is best to lovingly suggest other help for him. Prayer-counseling must be in a vertical direction, not only a horizontal one! You may be led to suggest he contact you again later on, when he or she feels ready for inner-healing prayer.

When Has the Work Been Completed?

How do you tell when your counselee doesn't need to come for more prayer? There needs to be agreement between counselors and counselee on this. The counselee may announce, "I don't have anything else to pray about." If this doesn't happen, and both counselors feel it's time to conclude, bring up the idea and see how the counselee responds. If he or she is hesitant, you might suggest, "Let's meet again in a month, and see how you're doing." If there's nothing much to pray about, you may conclude your time together with prayers of rejoicing, rehearsing the good things God has done. Keep the doors open, so that if the person wants to, he may return in a year or so. Ask the Holy Spirit to help you conclude the counseling series gently, so the counselee will not feel rejected. It would be better not to begin working with a person if you are going to drop him abruptly before he feels ready.

The person should by now have a pretty good idea how to pray for his or her own self. Don't forget that everyone you counsel becomes a potential counselor for someone else. Very often the counselee is already starting to pray with family members and others for healing, passing on the blessing.

After getting your feet wet reading these last two chapters, you may be wondering about other needs to pray about which haven't yet been mentioned. What about prayers for the depressed, the molested, the physically handicapped? It just so happens that's what the next chapter is about, so read on.

I will bless the Lord who counsels me. . . .
Psalms 16:7 TLB

6
Helps Along the Way

Because there are contrary opinions on teaching about the human *imagination,* I have shied away from using the word in connection with inner healing. Some secular magazine ads will assure you that if you will buy their special book you can develop your imagination in such a way as to make you wealthy, give you all the women (or men) you want to have affairs with, and make you an immediate success! Christians certainly don't want to have anything to do with such teachings, and so may mistakenly be fearful of anything that speaks of using the imagination.

True Meaning of "Imagination"

There are always counterfeits to keep us from the real. Imagination is not a naughty word, although non-Christian teachings may have caused Christians to be afraid of it. To avoid this problem, I have most often used the term *seeing by faith* taken from chapter 11 of Hebrews. This chapter tells how the faithful men and women in the Bible did great things, because they believed God's word to them, and, by faith, began to see or visualize what was promised, before they entered into the promise. This, by the way, is a pretty good description of what happens in soul-healing prayer, and is why I often use the term *seeing by faith.* Since some have a problem with the term *imagination,* it's good to have other ways of saying it. Use the term you feel most comfortable with and one that will not raise barriers.

The idea that imagination is somehow wicked comes from the fact that the translators of the King James Bible (and other translations, too) often used the word *imagination* to translate Hebrew words meaning "reasonings," "thought," "plans," and so forth, mainly in the negative sense of hostile, rebellious, or deceitful thoughts and plans. In this sense Genesis 6:5 and 8:21; Jeremiah 16:12 and 18:12; Proverbs 6:18 speak of "wicked imaginations." But the Scripture is not saying the ability to imagine is in itself wicked but that man uses this ability wickedly, just as he tends to misuse everything God has given him. Far from imagination being in itself wrong, it is God Himself who gives us the amazing ability to visualize, to imagine, that is, to make pictures in our minds, to conceive new things. This is in the very nature of spiritual beings.

But this imagination must be brought under obedience to God, and that is what I am talking about: inviting God to guide and use this ability to imagine that He has given us.

When we "see by faith" we are letting the Holy Spirit sanctify our imagination, bringing it up to the level of the Spirit. Your imagination or visual ability is a gift from God which can be used constructively or contaminated and used for evil. Proverbs says, "For as he thinks in his heart, so is he . . ." (23:7). And I add, as a man (or woman) thinks about other matters in his life, so they often become.

Another reason why some Christians don't like to use the word *imagination* is that they want to make sure what they're experiencing is not imaginary but real. Christians are sensitive to this, because the world already thinks we're on some kind of imaginary trip, believing in such things as: talking to an invisible God; trusting a special Book to give us God's direction for our lives, and planning to go to a place called heaven when we die.

I like what Dr. James Loder of Princeton Theological Seminary says in his book *The Transforming Moment* (Harper & Row, 1981): "The imaginative thought, act, or word puts you into history; the imaginary takes you out." For instance, if you have a friend who is imaginative, say, in interior decorating or in writing, you have a friend who has developed a God-given creative faculty. But if your friend lives in an imaginary world with imaginary friends, that's another matter!

Also, soul-healing prayer is not the same as such psychological exercises as *guided fantasy*, where a group, guided by a leader, imagines going on a journey or doing some other activity. I'm not saying it's wrong if a psychology class is being taught to release their creativity in this way, but that's not what we're talking about. In fact, we are careful not to attempt to program the person in what to see during prayer. As you will know by reading this book, we focus on Jesus and encourage the counselee to get in touch with that very real Person. We want to see whatever He has to show us during prayer. He is our Guide and we attempt to follow Him.

Good Vision

When on a journey it helps to have good vision. Yet the Bible doesn't say "according to your 'vision' be it unto you" but rather, according to your "faith" (Matthew 9:29 KJV). Yet visualizing and/or verbalizing is putting your faith into action. It gets God's promises from our heads into our hearts. This is what I see happening in soul-healing prayer. People who have believed and quoted Bible promises for years are appropriating them.

You will find three main levels of ability to "see by faith":

1. Some can visualize events clearly and easily. Some see the picture as in an abstract painting.

2. Some cannot see what is happening with their "mind's eye," but they can sense and feel what is happening.

3. Some cannot visualize at all, but they can verbalize what is happening.

Things you can say to help are: "If you can't see Jesus in the scene, can you by faith sense He is there?" "Just make a word picture if you can't see the scene." Whether the person can visualize, sense, or verbalize, these are all ways to exercise faith and they will bear fruit. It's good to allow God to work in all areas:

The most important thing is for him or her to be aware of God's presence when praying.

Things That May Block a Person's Prayer and "Seeing by Faith"

1. Hasn't taken the first step of forgiving from the will.

2. Present scene is too hard to pray about. Need to start with an easier one.

3. Needs healing with earthly father relationship, so it's hard to see or feel Jesus with him (or her).

4. May be angry with God and blaming Him. We can't have a meaningful conversation with someone we're angry with, without being reconciled first.

5. May have a fresh hurt which must be healed before praying about anything else.

6. May be in bondage to cults and occult practices of the past if such beliefs haven't been fully renounced.

7. Needs practice in allowing childlike quality of visualizing to be renewed through prayer.

Those Who Can't Emote

Some people find it difficult to express their emotions easily. Don't be concerned about this, or express concern to your counselee about it. God will still be able to heal, though it may not show at first.

God will use every means possible to heal, although the signs of healing may be indirect. A person may begin to evidence emotional healing in dreams before he or she is aware of it while awake. One man we know was schooled never to show his emotions, and to regard any man who cried in public as a sentimental weakling. He had been especially taught not to express emotion about his religion.

This man strongly resisted visualizing Jesus coming to him and expressing love for him. "I love Jesus," he said, "but I can't imagine Him coming and putting His arms around me, and I'm not sure I want Him to!" He could not remember ever having his parents hug him or take him on their laps, although they were loving people. They, too, had been taught to inhibit their show of affection in most ways. "I always kissed my mom or dad when going away somewhere, or going to bed, but I don't remember any hugging or caressing," says our friend. "The only time I shed tears," he said, "is when I felt sorry for myself, or in anger or frustration."

He now has a loving wife, and gets plenty of love and affection in his marriage, but still has a hard time expressing his feelings about God. After a few sessions of healing prayer, this man began to *dream* he was weeping uncontrollably, not from sorrow or self-pity, but because he was feeling such strong love for God! This has happened now two or three times. He still finds it difficult to express or feel emotion in his waking life much of the time, but he's much easier to pray with now than at first, and he says, "I know something's happening. I'm loosening up inside! Praise the Lord!"

Sometimes inner-healing prayer brings immediate and dramatic results, and at other times it's a slow process, or the results may be more indirect and subtle. One person described it this way: "It's like I'd had a dull headache for years, and one morning I woke up and realized it was gone." Some healing prayer simply gives a person the ability to make right and clear choices. Others are enabled to love themselves, others, and God more deeply or for the first time. Some have basic changes in the underlying attitudes and patterns of their lives. The man we spoke of as having difficulty expressing his emotions also is experiencing a deep attitude change. He says, "Even though I have known Jesus most of my life, and been baptized in the Holy Spirit for nearly a quarter century, I still had a deep underlying attitude which said, 'Look out! Things are going to get worse as time goes by!' I was basically depressive in my outlook, and very negative. Now, after receiving inner healing, my basic attitude is changing to one of optimism, and looking ahead with joyful anticipation. It's so real, it's hard to believe, but it's true!"

Specific Prayer Helps

The following are examples of various prayer needs you may encounter, together with some specific ways the Holy Spirit has led when praying for these things. Please read the whole series before beginning to use them; the information builds from one to the next, so I do not have to repeat myself. Don't begin by just dipping in here and there. Of necessity these instructions are brief, sort of like directions on road signs. These are not meant to be rules, so don't feel you must follow them exactly. Follow Him.

The Strong-Willed Inner Child. The strong-willed person is often difficult to pray with because it's hard for him to submit to another person. Even though he wants help, getting him to pray may be a battle of wills. If you encounter this problem, try having him pray this prayer, following you phrase by phrase, before beginning:

> Dear God, I'm here because I want Your help. I thank You for giving me a strong will which has been helpful many times, but I also know it must be submitted to You so I can be healed. I do now submit my will to You and ask You to soften me, so I can receive Your help through those You've sent to help me. In Jesus' name.

As you get to know the strong-willed person you will see that he probably needed such a will in order to survive, and you will understand him better. Yet, what was a necessity at one time will now be a hindrance to growth, if not yielded to God. Use this prayer again preceding other inner-healing prayers. Remember too, that not everyone who needs help is ready to receive it.

The Dyslexic. A dyslexic person has difficulty in reading and understanding words. As a child he may have seen words (or numbers) backwards, or upside down. Or perhaps he has auditory dyslexia, which means he has difficulty grasping the meaning of something that is said to him, unless it is repeated. He or she may have had a great struggle with this in school.

Marsha Stockdill, a prayer-counseling leader at Resurrection Episcopal Church in Bellevue, Washington, says, "Dyslexic people are often very creative, but have a hard time getting in touch with their feelings. In inner-healing prayer they are more apt to *see* a scene than *feel* it, although the latter comes quite easily and with great relief when praying more times."

If the problem hasn't been caught and helped in early childhood, you will need to pray about embarrassment—especially in school. As Marsha indicates, dyslexic people normally find it easy to visualize. (Reread *Emotionally Free,* chapter 2.)

Depression. Major feeling: This is not as much an emotion as a shutdown of the emotions. His eyes may look tired and lifeless, and shoulders may be slumped.

Depression is often caused by hurts from others, which have not or cannot be expressed, so the person has turned the anger in upon himself. There are many kinds of depression, but we're mainly concerned with those that stem from childhood hurts. Where he can express his present feelings, ask if he can remember when he had these same feelings in his childhood and have him tell you about it.

Do not tell jokes or try to cheer him up or tell him to try harder. ". . . weep with those who weep" (Romans 12:15). The prayer-counselor needs to encourage the counselee to talk about his hurts. You might ask when he first remembers being depressed and explore the circumstances at that time. Take a few minutes to share if you have been depressed, and tell how you came out of it, giving him hope. Don't tell him he doesn't have enough faith. Let him know he can count on you to have faith for him. Tell him not to be concerned if he doesn't *feel* any different right away. You, the counselor, must show confidence and be definite about being able to help.

If the depression is too deep, and he is too debilitated to pray himself, the prayer partners may need to allow him to simply rest while they do the praying. Self-hate may be at the root of the problem. Like the example of the young woman whose will was crushed, the Holy Spirit may lead you to pray a Creative Prayer in which Jesus is seen putting a new light within him or increasing his dim, flickering pilot light, into a brighter radiance (Psalms 18:28, 29). Some depression has. physical causes; work with the counselee as you search for the answers together, and encourage a medical exam if the depression does not seem to respond to inner-healing prayer.

If the person is suicidal, check with your pastor for guidance or referral. (For further information review "Release From Depression," page 147, in *Emotionally Free*.) If referral is indicated, offer to work with the counselee and therapist if desired. This reduces the risk of communicating rejection to the counselee, and even with therapy a supportive relationship can be helpful.

Temper Tantrums. The counselee should observe what situation precedes uncontrollable temper, for instance, repeated unfair treatment. *Temper tantrums can be turned to good when you look at them to help pinpoint direction for prayer.* Each situation connected with being treated unfairly should be prayed about, Reliving the Scene With Jesus. The Hurt Inner Child may need further healing, so other childhood scenes may need to be prayed about also.

Anorexia. Description: Feels fat even when underweight; when eating has strange food rituals; dislike for how the body looks; self-hate; low self-esteem; a need to feel in control; fears rejection and failure.

Anorexia is a dramatic weight loss from consistent self-starvation or from severe self-imposed dieting. Women, especially teens and young adults, have this problem. Though fewer in number, some men are also affected.

Pray for scenes where people embarrassed her, or caused her not to feel good about herself. Through prayer, she needs to receive much comforting love from Jesus.

Often the young anorexic does not want to grow up, but to remain small. It would be good to pray about prenatal times and any trauma there. (See list in the next chapter.) Also pray about a resistance to being born—trying to gain control of the situation when being forced out of the womb into the world. It's important, too, to pray about the first two years of life, when the child should have been learning to trust people. For more information, read *Starving for Attention,* listed in the bibliography. See also chapter 12 in *Emotionally Free.*

The Alcoholic. Description: The alcoholic feels inadequate, is in psychological pain, and wants to escape from that pain and from life. He fears relating to people; feels like an outsider—as if he came from another planet; often compares himself to others, feeling they are more capable.

Carolyn Budd, a prayer-counselor in Arcadia, California, who has worked with alcoholics, points out that the Twelve Steps of Alcoholics Anonymous and their Fourth Step Inventory can be good preparation for forgiveness and inner-healing prayer. You can get this material from Alcoholics Anonymous in your community. She also says that although alcoholism is a physical problem in that the person's body reacts abnormally to alcohol, predisposition to alcoholism comes in part from emotional hurts. Alcoholism is also related to nutritional deficiency which the person attempts to correct by turning to alcohol, of course, only aggravating the condition. It is a disease of both mind and body.

The alcoholic often has a Hurt Inner Child, so this would be a good place to start praying. If the alcoholic's mother was alcoholic, prenatal prayers are in order, since the child could have suffered physical effects from alcohol in the mother's bloodstream before birth. There could have been emotional upheaval from the many problems alcoholism would have caused the mother, which the child could have sensed while still in the womb. The effects of alcohol on the unborn child, called *alcohol fetal syndrome,* can range from mild, all the way to retardation and deformity.

You might keep in mind that the alcoholic's spouse and children may need healing from the effect of abusive language and from bad memories.

Physical Handicaps. Pray about the beginning of the physical problem: the scene of the accident, or the emotional trauma at the discovery of a serious disease. If the person is deformed from birth, pray prenatal and birth prayers (see next chapter). The Holy Spirit may give you or the counselee a word of knowledge about a very early hurt beyond conscious memory. Follow God's leadings. It's more important to be psychologically whole than physically whole, but God wants both. Sometimes physical healing takes place as we pray for healing of the soul.

Helps in Praying for Various Traumas

I want to say a word about guilt before we look at the lists of traumatic problems. A Christian should not have real guilt in his life any longer than it takes to repent from the cause of that guilt. The only reason for guilt is *sin;* the remedy is *repentance.* If the sin has been repented of and the person still feels guilty, that is *false guilt.* False guilt may be effectively handled through inner-healing prayer. A guilt trip occurs when we think we have to work to *earn* forgiveness from God, instead of receiving it as the free gift it is.

Divorced Person. Major feeling: rejection. If the spouse initiated the divorce, the person's major feeling will be rejection. Go to the scene when the divorce was asked for, or papers served, or, if applicable, go to the scene where he or she discovered the mate's unfaithfulness. Let the hurt out with Jesus there to comfort. It is possible that the person's relationship with his or her parent of the opposite sex may be affecting relationships with others of the same gender—that is, if a girl did not have a good relationship with her father, she may have problems relating to all males.

Divorce Initiator. Major feeling: guilt. Where the person was the initiator of the divorce, even though he or she may consider the action justified, the major feeling is usually guilt. Whether or not the guilt feeling is valid, after repentance, if he or she still feels guilt, that is *false guilt.* Inner-healing prayer for memories leading up to and surrounding the divorce will help to heal this.

Memories of a Suicide. This refers to a person who needs to pray about the memory of a parent (or close friend) who committed suicide and calls for special wisdom and sensitivity on the part of the counselors. The counselee will eventually need to forgive the person for taking his or her life. *Review any good or simply positive scenes with the parent or other person, before praying about the suicide memory. Do not be tempted to judge where the person has gone at death; leave such matters with God.* If the person experienced disillusionment with the parent before his or her death, pray about that scene before the memory of the suicide.

Caution in Regard to Suicide. If a person you are trying to help is actually threatening suicide, unless you yourself are trained in handling this kind of crisis, get help right away from your pastor, or another professional person in the community who can deal with it. Don't assume he doesn't mean anything by his threats. There is a mistaken idea that if a person talks about suicide, he's not going to do it. That is tragically untrue.

On the other hand, there are many people who have thoughts of self-destruction from time to time, due to depression, or other hurts in the soul. You don't have to drop a counselee because he admits to having or having had such thoughts, provided he is not actually threatening to harm himself. Inner healing can dramatically alter such feelings, and drive away these thoughts permanently.

After the Death of a Loved One. Emotions: guilt for mistakes (not usually real guilt), regrets. Have counselee talk about or relive one or more happy scenes. Go to a scene near the time of death, and if he wasn't able to be with the person at death or attend the funeral, ask Jesus to help him say "good-bye" there, or feel a good-bye in his heart. He may relive with Jesus the scenes before the funeral or at the funeral, letting God comfort and support him. Have a prayer of relinquishment of the person:

"Into your hands, Lord, I commend his [or her] spirit. I will no longer try to pretend he hasn't died or try to live as though he were here. I choose to release the pain involved in these memories. Help me to think about and rejoice in the happy memories. Thank You, Lord Jesus."

Miscarriage. Emotions: grief, and sometimes misplaced anger at God. Have the mother relive the hurtful scene or scenes with Jesus.

Often in prayer Jesus is seen taking the child to be with Him. Be very sure the mother (or father) doesn't see God as the One who caused the loss of the child.

The parents may want to choose a name for the child they trust is now growing up in God's kingdom, and whom they hope to meet there one day. They may want to sent their child a gift of love through Jesus. In some instances, the parents may need to forgive the doctor, others, or even (they may think) God.

Abortion. Emotion: guilt. (We're not here to judge whether a person should feel guilty or not; or whether abortion is ever justified, as in where the mother's life is in danger, but experience in prayer has shown that some guilt is present.) Distinguish between true and false guilt. If necessary, lead the person to a confession of the real guilt, and assure her (or him—fathers can be involved, too) of God's forgiveness. If she still feels guilty, that is false guilt, and means she thinks she still has to earn God's forgiveness. Be very careful not to pass judgment, and so load on more false guilt. You are there to love and heal.

Pray about the actual scene of abortion, reliving it with Jesus. Counselee often needs to forgive self, father of the child, doctor, others. Suggest the same kind of prayers about seeing Jesus taking the child to be with Him as were given in the case of miscarriage. Sometimes mothers and fathers have, through Jesus, asked the child's forgiveness.

If there were several abortions, usually the first one needs prayer initially, and the others may automatically be healed at the same time, or you may find you need to have prayer for them individually.

Rape or Molestation. Feelings: humiliation, shame, memories of pain, sometimes guilt (usually false guilt). *In prayer, you encourage the counselee to come into the scene where Jesus comes in.* It's not necessary to relive the details of a violent scene in order to be healed; the counselee will usually see Jesus there to comfort and heal after the fact. However, be sure to follow Jesus' leading. Sometimes after Reliving the Scene With Jesus Prayer, in the next session you may have a Creative Prayer, seeing events as God would have wanted them. Creative Prayer here isn't always necessary, but if more help is needed with traumatic memories it may help. When the counselee is able, she should be encouraged to speak forgiveness to the attacker, in the first person present tense, and then perhaps pray for his salvation.

Sometimes, when a person experiences a sexual trauma such as rape or molestation, without healing prayer and the forgiveness it brings, he or she is left open to the enemy's sending further emissaries at later dates to increase the psychological injury. Prayer is the best deterrent. In such cases, after healing prayer, it's good to pray against a seducing spirit which may still be working to keep the person vulnerable. If married, the husband (or wife) may also benefit from prayer.

Rapist. Feeling: aggression against women; at times obsessed with hate. Presumably guilt has already been dealt with through repentance and confession, and restitution made where possible, but the person may still need help forgiving himself. *He especially needs healing with mother or mother substitute, and then also other women who hurt him, so he will be able to forgive them.* Often a man with this kind of background will have a battered wife who also needs healing. However, the greatest gift to her is her husband's healing.

Incest. Feelings: helplessness, depression, humiliation, burdened, anger, guilt (usually false guilt). Occurs most often with a father, stepfather, grandfather (and sometimes a mother), or other parent substitutes. Mothers sometimes are aware of the problem but often fear doing anything about it.

The situation may have gone on for years, but the most traumatic memories to pray about are the first encounters, then any others that stand out in the memory. If the victim feels some guilt (real or false), perhaps because at times he did enjoy the incestuous relationship, help him or her confess it to God, and then you may say something such as:

"God's Word says, 'If you confess your sins, He is faithful and just to forgive you your sins and to cleanse you from all unrighteousness'" (1 John 1:9, *paraphrased*). It's often good for the counselor (or counselors) to lay a hand upon the counselee's head while giving this scriptural assurance. If the counselee needs more assurance she (or he) should be encouraged to see a minister or priest.

Near the end or during a Reliving the Scene Prayer, the counselee often spontaneously sees a creative scene, such as a fountain, a spar-

kling stream, or river in which he or she is bathed. One woman saw
Jesus leading her into a pool of water. She went under the water
seven times, once for each of the seven times she was attacked. The
Holy Spirit's picture gives the person a wonderful feeling of clean-
ness and purity. (This kind of creative scene is experienced with the
person raped outside the family as well as within it.)

Through prayer, forgiveness needs to be spoken to the guilty parent, the passive parent who could have stopped it, and to self for not
knowing what to do—at least often not until much later.

Masturbation. Feelings: unloved, frustrated, guilt (real or false). Dr.
Jim Dobson, Christian psychologist, in his film series *Focus on the
Family* estimates that in the U.S. 95 percent of males and 50 percent
of females have experienced masturbation. It is immature sexuality,
and if the person does not grow out of it, it can be a habit which ex-
cludes the mate after marriage. It's the childish idea, "I can be
everything to myself. I don't need anyone else." It's a drawing
within oneself for comfort. The Bible is silent on the subject. The
story of Onan in Genesis 38 is often cited as an example of masturbation; in fact, it is often termed *Onanism.* If you read the chapter
you will see without question that Onan's act was one of *co-
itus interruptus,* not masturbation, and that his sin was that, in the
patriarchal system, having been required to marry the widow of his
deceased brother, he wanted to avoid fathering a child which he
knew would not be reckoned as his, but his brother's. Masturbation
doesn't come into the issue at all.

*Be tender with the person who reveals this problem as he (or she)
may think this is the worst sin of all.* Excessive masturbation is a
symptom of deep needs, especially of acceptance and love. The
person doesn't need to be judged, but to be healed.

Reliving the Scene Prayer may begin at the time when he first
experimented, or was taught by a peer. The person will benefit from
Creative Prayer in building happy memories into his childhood. He
or she needs to forgive self and/or others.

The enemy loves to connect masturbation with escape into a fantasy world, so that the sexual gratification provides a "payoff" for
going that way. In fantasy, the person may see him or herself in a
wrong sexual relationship: premarital, extramarital, homosexual,
and so forth. In such an instance deliverance prayer may be needed.

Again, see chapter 15, "Deliverance Brings Healing," in *Emotionally Free* to review a specific way to pray about fantasy.

Homosexual Experience and Memories. Feelings: confused identity, inadequacy, rejection, guilt (if the person has repented, the guilt is false), and so forth. Many claim this problem can be hereditary, and therefore not only incurable, but a "valid life-style." I do not wish to pass judgment on this or any other human problem, but the persons I have prayed with had clearly been programmed to it by past hurts, and these were healed. Dave, whose account was given in *Emotionally Free,* was set up for an identity problem before birth. *What we're praying about here is the person who had a sexual encounter with the same sex, willingly or unwillingly, and then desired and participated further in such acts.*

(A person should not be labeled homosexual simply because he or she shows physical traits of the opposite sex, or seems to have extreme need for affection from his or her own sex. Such extreme emotional hunger is often because the person's inner child is still looking for a parent's love and this need can be met through prayer.)

Pray about the initial homosexual experience, Reliving the Scene With Jesus, remembering to come in where Jesus leads you in; where His presence can be seen or felt; and then pray for other experiences which the Holy Spirit brings to mind. I am told the late Agnes Sanford would pray and ask that the person's sexual energy and desires be rechanneled into their normal course. That sounds good to me. Then use Creative Prayer to build happy childhood memories. Prenatal prayer here may be very important; see chapter 11 in *Emotionally Free.*

Leanne Payne, author and teacher, who often deals with the healing of sexual identity, gives further prayers and insights in her excellent book *The Broken Image,* which will help anyone wanting further information.

Other Kinds of Prayer I've Found Helpful

Breaking Wrong Soul Ties. I first learned the importance of breaking wrong soul ties from Wayne Butchart, experienced missionary and Bible teacher. I found that people's souls can be knit together for blessing or for bondage. A husband and wife in a good marriage have a healthy soul tie which is important. Jonathan and David were best friends, and Scripture describes their souls as knit together (1 Samuel 18:1). But wrong soul ties can so control a person that they can't function as they should on either a natural or spiritual level. Through a simple prayer, these can be broken.

There are various kinds of wrong psychic or soul ties:

1. *A person may be tied to a possessive mother or father or parent substitute who tries to control him long after he is an adult and on his own.* You may want to use the symbolism of cutting a psychological umbilical cord. The person will feel *more* love for the parent or parent figure after being set free.

2. *If the person has had a premarital or extramarital love affair, he may still be psychologically tied to the person with whom he had the affair.* Point out that in breaking such ties he is not rejecting the real affection or appreciation he may have had, and that if that person is in Christ, they will meet again in heaven, where their friendship can safely continue.

3. *Bonds need to be broken with anyone to whom through witchcraft or any other occult or cultish practice he has yielded his will.*

After the counselee realizes with whom he has a wrong bond, and before praying, have him visualize where he feels the person's attachment to be: intellectual (would be the head); emotional (would be the heart); sexual (the abdomen); manipulative (the hands); a drawing in the wrong direction (the feet); and so forth. Tell him that when you pray this wrong tie will be broken. During prayer, sometimes the person actually feels a physical release. Have him pray together with you something like this:

> In the name of Jesus I acknowledge a wrong soul tie between myself and _____. The Scripture says, the yoke shall be broken because of the anointing (Isaiah 10:27); and God's anointing abides in His people (1 John 2:27). I take the sword of the Spirit now and cut this wrong psychic tie, in Jesus' name and under the protection of His blood. *Amen.*

Remind him of Galatians 5:1: "When Christ freed us, he meant us to remain free. Stand firm, therefore, and do not submit again to the yoke of slavery" (JERUSALEM). This is a good verse to claim to keep the tie from being reestablished. After breaking the soul tie, the person may need further inner healing.

Please note that I'm not speaking here of having a soul tie to a person who has departed this life. The kind of tie I've been talking about would presumably be broken by death. There is, however, a kind of influence that can extend from generation to generation. Let's talk about this next.

Breaking Harmful Generation Ties. There can be destructive patterns in family lines—physical weaknesses, ways of thinking and attitudes that have been passed along, or spiritual influences, such as witchcraft or other occult practices. Go back three generations to the great-grandparents. If possible, name each person at each generation level (if you don't know the names, just say "my great-grandfather on my mother's side" and so forth. Then by faith, place the cross of Jesus and blood of Jesus between each generation, as a barrier to the passing along of any wrong influences and to break any wrong ties. You may also want to do this between yourself and your own offspring, for their protection. (Read chapter 13 in *Emotionally Free* for further review.)

Helps in Forgiving

Before praying for inner healing, you will have asked the counselee to forgive all those who have hurt him in the past. This is at the level of the will. At the end of Reliving the Scene With Jesus you will have directed him to forgive, as from the time the hurt occurred. There are other areas where forgiveness may be needed.

Forgiving Himself. If the counselee has difficulty forgiving himself, ask if he would be as unforgiving to another person as he is being to himself. Have him pray about the unhealed memory. Then have him speak forgiveness to *himself:*

> [His own name], I forgive you; I won't hold this against you any longer. God has forgiven and forgotten long ago, and it's wrong not to believe His Word. I will hold this against myself no longer. In Jesus' name.

Forgiving God. A person who is having difficulty forgiving God the Father (it's more often the Father than the Son) needs to work in two directions: 1) to forgive his earthly father; and, 2) to understand the Fall of man and God's plan for restoration. To assist with the second part, I highly recommend the first two chapters of *Moving Right Along in the Spirit*.

Encourage him to tell God exactly how he feels. God can handle it! God is big enough to handle such rejection. Then let him pray something like this:

> Dear Father, if there's anything I have to forgive You for, it's loving so much that You gave us human beings free wills that we could either bless or destroy with. I've sometimes blamed You mistakenly for what the enemy or others under his direction have done. Please forgive me, and thank You that these barriers I put up between us are removed. Thank You for Your continuing mercy and love. In Jesus' name.

Forgiving at the Cross. Sometimes it's easier to forgive a person when we can visualize Jesus doing it first. Of course it was done once and for all nearly two thousand years ago, but in prayer it can be made more real for the present. Have the counselee picture Jesus on the cross, with the person needing forgiveness and himself standing at the foot of the cross. See and hear Jesus say, "Father, forgive them; for they know not what they do . . ." (Luke 23:34 KJV). Then visualize Jesus speaking to the guilty person, "John, I forgive *you*."

Now you yourself forgive as Jesus did. "Father, I forgive [name] for he [or she] didn't truly know what he was doing or he wouldn't have done it. I forgive you now [name] through Jesus Christ, and in His name I pray." You can vary this prayer as the Lord leads.

Forgiving a Group. I first heard this kind of prayer on a tape recording of Father John H. Hampsch, a Roman Catholic priest, who is active in inner healing. I have used a modified version of it several times, especially when the counselee had a large number of people to forgive in a particular scene, such as in an accident.

See a room as big as you need it to be. Let the people enter the room, beginning with the person you're having the biggest problem forgiving, then the next and the next. When everyone is there, wait to see or feel Jesus enter. See Him giving you strength first, and then, with Him present by your side, go to each person and speak forgiveness. It's not important that they ask you to forgive them;

you are expressing unconditional forgiveness—the kind of forgiveness Jesus gave and continues to give us. In the process, any time you need extra help from Jesus, stop and receive it before you go on. This prayer can be used either for forgiving from the *will* at the beginning of inner-healing prayer, or at the end, when forgiving from the *emotions.*

I hope some of these ideas will help you as you pray for people in need, and for yourself. These are only suggestions for prayer; please do not lean any less on the Holy Spirit for His guidance because you have these helps. The main way I learned these things was through praying with others and seeking God's directions for their immediate needs. We are to pray not simply by well thought-out plans, though this is good, but by responding to situations as they are encountered in prayer.

As you come better to understand people and their experiences, and pray with them, your love for them will grow. Remember these words from Coleridge's "Ancient Mariner":

> He prayeth best who loveth best. . . .

Here's some thought-provoking verse on the need of showing mercy to others along the way.

> Pray don't find fault with the man who limps
>   Or stumbles along the road,
> Unless you have worn the shoes he wears
>   Or struggled beneath his load.
>
> There may be tacks in his shoes that hurt,
>   Though hidden away from view,
> Or the burden he bears, placed on your back,
>   Might cause you to stumble, too.
>
> Don't sneer at the man who's down today,
>   Unless you have felt the blow
> That caused his fall or felt the shame
>   That only the fallen know.
>
> You may be strong, but still the blows
>   That were his, if dealt to you
> In the selfsame way at the selfsame time,
>   Might cause you to stagger, too.

AUTHOR UNKNOWN

For unto us a Child is born, Unto us a Son is given; And the government will be upon His shoulder. And His name will be called Wonderful, Counselor, Mighty God, Everlasting Father, Prince of Peace.

Isaiah 9:6

7
Journey to Life's Beginning

Through Jesus and the power of the Spirit experienced at our new birth, it is possible to have memories before or at physical birth healed—restoring damaged places in our souls. As the unborn or newborn child's emotions within us are given what was lacking, they accept Jesus' love, rather than continuing to hold on to the pain. Then we as adults are enabled to forgive.

Because of Jesus' birth
there's healing available for your birth.

Barbara Kehs, an effective prayer counselor at the Cathedral of Saint Philip, Atlanta, wrote to us following a seminar,

I want to tell you that *nothing* has helped our inner healing counseling as much as learning to pray from the moment of conception, thru the fetal period and birth process. We are grateful for these insights. God is certainly moving in more powerful ways as we use creative prayers, and our Lord ministers to each person in truly unique and individual ways. What a blessing to just be a *part* of this ministry!

In soul-healing ministry we pray about each stage of life, but mostly we find ourselves praying about childhood. The reason for this is that adult hurts are often related to childhood hurts, and our childhood memories are the earliest we can recall. Root causes are most important for the deepest healing. Often the deepest roots to a problem are in prenatal or birth memories or in infancy. Since these memories are stored in the subconscious, they are not easy to get at. Fortunately, we don't have to consciously remember everything to be healed from it. As we are open to God's gifts and guidance, we can be sure He will reveal what we need to know, if and when we need to know it.

As you begin soul-healing ministry your prayers will usually be about *childhood memories, then teens and adulthood.* Later, when you feel ready, you may want to pray for *these earliest times.* I prayed with people for inner healing for a year before praying my first prenatal or birth prayer. The idea was new to me. I've learned a lot since then and realize there's more to learn.

At a seminar for the Anglican Church in Singapore I was asked: "What type of problem leads you to know that a person needs prenatal or birth prayer?"

The French obstetrician Frederick Leboyer says that *all* births are traumatic. If this is so, then everybody might benefit from prenatal prayer. Here we're concerned, though, with extra complications your counselee may have experienced either before or at birth, such as:

Birth Complications

Long, hard labor for mother and child; breech birth; umbilical cord wrapped around the neck; delivered by instrument; born prematurely or by cesarean section—here he missed the alternate compression and stimulation he or she should have experienced in the birth process, comparable to breaking the egg to let the chick out, instead of letting it break its own way out. Effect of these missing factors can be supplied in healing prayer. If he had an Rh blood factor problem; if for any reason he was separated from his mother at birth: left alone while mother was being tended to for excessive hemorrhage, and so forth; put in an incubator, or had surgery immediately after birth, or if the mother died at the birth.

If he felt rejected at the time of his first breast feeding; if mother or father registered immediate disappointment with his or her sex; if the mother suffered severe trauma or consistent fear while carrying him; if he was blamed for his mother's illness or near or actual death from giving birth; if his parents contemplated aborting him; if his mother smoked (with each inhalation cutting off some of his oxygen); if his mother was an alcoholic (when the mother was inebriated the child could have felt dizzy, confused, and ill); if his mother had to be away from him for several months in his early infancy; if he had a twin, and the other baby died; if he was constricted in the womb during prenatal life; if he was born out of wedlock, especially if his father or mother refused him; if he was an unwanted child. All these represent needs for prayer.

Symptoms That Show a Person Needs Prayer

He has claustrophobia (fear of being in a small place), and especially if he can't stand the thought of having been in his mother's womb; if he has fear of, or often dreams of falling; if he has an insatiable need to be hugged; if he has a death wish, perhaps manifested by a disease which has no medical reason; if he is obsessed with women's breasts; if he was a twin and from birth felt overshadowed by his double.

A woman needs prayer if she hated being pregnant, and especially if she had trouble loving her baby after birth. (Share with her that, when healed and able, she may pray for her child's own prenatal times and birth even before the little one understands and/or when the child is older.)

(*A Disclaimer.* In the following prayers for prenatal and early memories, we're not talking about hypnotic regression, or any kind of psychological manipulation. We are simply praying as the Holy Spirit leads.)

Before You Pray

Good preparatory reading for prenatal and birth prayer are *The Secret Life of the Unborn Child,* by psychiatrist Thomas Verny and John Kelly; and *Birth Without Violence* by French obstetrician Frederick Leboyer. A book with marvelous pictures, and especially good to use before praying with a school-age child, is *A Child is Born* by obstetrician Axel Ingleman-Sundberg and Claes Wirsens.

Whether the counselee reads these books or not, I highly recommend them to those going into consistent soul-healing ministry. [*They're not required reading before a seminar.*]

As always, the counselee's best preparation and the counselor's best guidance for prayer is a knowledge of Scripture. In *Emotionally Free* I give the Scriptures in the order the Lord inspired them to me for prenatal praying, month by month, together with *Creative Prenatal and Birth Prayers.* A very brief overview and the Scripture references follow. Be sure to review chapter 11 in *Emotionally Free.* I especially like the translations of the Scriptures I chose there.

Have the counselee read over these Scriptures especially before, and if possible after, your prayer time together.

Scriptures for Each Month

Conception
Hear Him call your name. You are chosen.

Isaiah 49:1
Ephesians 1:4
John 10:3

First Month
His presence covered you in your mother's womb.

Psalms 139:13

Second Month
God approved of you and is happy with your sexual identity.

Jeremiah 1:5
Isaiah 44:2

Third Month
Praise God for the miracle of your creation.

Psalms 139:14

Fourth Month
God quickened you, gave you life. Thank Him.

1 Timothy 6:13

Fifth Month
If you felt your mother's fears, receive healing. Thank God for your mother and life and nourishment received through her.

1 John 4:18

Sixth Month

You were anointed top to toe with protective ointment (*vernix caseosa*) and spiritually you are anointed.

Luke 1:44
Psalms 23:5

Seventh Month

By the middle of this month all parts of your body are completed. God is preparing you for birth.

Psalms 139:15, 16

Eighth Month

God's presence is there and He's getting you and your mother ready for the process of birth.

Isaiah 66:12, 13

Ninth Month

As you move out of the dark birth canal, the light of Jesus draws you to Him. He delivers you, cleans you off, and presents you to His Father.

John 16:21
Psalms 22:9, 10
Galatians 1:15

For the Adopted

God loves you and adopts you for His child.

Isaiah 49:15, 16
Psalms 27:10
Psalms 68:5

Getting Ready to Pray

Ask the counselee about his (or her) prenatal times and birth. Find out if anything in these previous listed categories fits his picture. Maybe he doesn't know much about his beginning (many people don't), and his parents are deceased. Even so, if you feel the Holy Spirit indicating prenatal prayer, and the person is willing, go ahead and pray. It isn't necessary to know the details, and God will reveal what you need to know as you go along.

It's helpful to have a special area of need in mind before you begin. You don't have to pray through the entire conception, nine months in the womb, and birth memories, the first time you pray, although it's not uncommon to do so. You do eventually want to cover the complete cycle. If the situation at conception is the most painful memory, you may want to start at birth and work backwards to conception before you complete the prayers. You can stop and start again when you need to. As in my illustration of Dave (*Emotionally Free*, pages 160–162), at times God may supernaturally put you into a prayer for a prenatal or birth scene when you're not expecting it.

What to Find Out Before You Pray

1. What did your counselee like to be called when he was a child? There's much importance in a name.
2. Was he a full-term baby? If not, you will want to pray the right number of months and revise your prayer accordingly.
3. Where was he born? Hospital? Home?
4. Were there any special complications with his birth?
5. Who was there at his birth? Where was his father?
6. Who delivered him? Doctor, midwife, father?
7. What did he weigh?

When You Pray

1. Have a quiet, peaceful atmosphere and help the counselee feel comfortable.

2. Have the person put anything out of his (or her) hands or off his lap. He should close his eyes so he can concentrate and his mind won't wander. (To help children close their eyes I explain their eyelids are like a screen which needs to be pulled down, so God can project on it the good pictures He has for them to see.)

3. You and your prayer partner may sit in the usual semicircle but be flexible. When praying about early times, one young woman only felt comfortable when she had her head in my lap. The Holy Spirit will lead you.

4. Encourage the person to relax.

5. If during prayer the person responds emotionally, remind him or her: "God's presence is with you in your mother's womb. Everything is going to be all right"; or whatever else the Holy Spirit prompts you to say. Remind him it's a memory which God is healing. You may be led to put your arm around him and rock him as Laura and I did, with her husband, Dave, until he stopped crying; or you may stop for a while, ask what's happening, and then pray more specifically.

6. If he drops off to sleep, which may happen in praying for these early times, you may continue, since the human spirit and subconscious are receptive anyway, and after all, a child does a lot of sleeping before birth. However, if every time you pray for prenatal times or birth the counselee goes to sleep, he may be escaping because the material is too difficult to pray about right now. Pray about other things and come back to this later.

7. Encourage the counselee to stop and share what he sees or feels during prayer, even if it doesn't make sense. When the Lord reveals subconscious infant memories, they often don't make sense to our adult minds.

8. At the end of the prayer time, be sure to ask what the person saw and/or felt while praying, if he hasn't yet expressed it. Further understanding may come some time later.

It may take several meetings with your counselee to complete the full cycle of these prenatal and birth prayers.

Specific Offenses to Forgive

Conception. Forgive parents if born out of wedlock.

Sexual identity at the end of second month. Encourage acceptance of self for Jesus' sake. Have Him let you know if there's any problem in doing this. Forgive parents if they wanted the opposite sex.

If nearly aborted, forgive parent, parents, and doctor at that time.

If child felt unwanted and consequently didn't want to be born, as from before his birth—have him forgive his parents and ask God's forgiveness for not wanting to be born.

If the doctor, midwife, or father didn't handle the birth process correctly, speak forgiveness to him or her.

If your mother didn't want to hold you or feed you at first, forgive her.

You may find others to add to this list.

How to Pray, Using Creative Scripture Prayers

The scriptural order for praying from conception to birth, and the very detailed series of Scripture-based prayers for the nine months in the womb, and for the birth experience, are to be used here. They're found beginning on page 173 in *Emotionally Free.* These Creative Prayers can be used in various ways. You may want to read them to the counselee while he's praying; or tape-record them and pray together while you both listen; or, most effective, use the prayers as a model and pray aloud with the counselee as the Holy Spirit leads.

Other ways to use the *Creative Scripture Prayers:*

1. A pregnant woman can pray them for her unborn child month by month.

2. You may pray them with a woman who's fearful in her pregnancy. Pray both for the mother and the unborn child.

3. If a woman had a difficult pregnancy, these prayers will help her. She may actually have picked up her negative feelings about being pregnant from her mother's feelings about pregnancy before the daughter was born.

4. A mother can pray with her infant while he or she is still in the womb, or too young to understand what she's doing.

5. The mother (and father) can pray for the child when he (or she) is old enough to wonder about the beginning of life. Show the child pictures in *A Child Is Born,* and also give him a few Scriptures as preparation for prayer, especially Psalms 139:13.

Fathers Can Pray, Too

It's good for a father to sing to, talk to, and pray for the baby before birth. Here's a prayer for a father to pray as he lays hands on the baby and the mother, especially during the last trimester of pregnancy:

> Through Jesus I speak to you, my child. Your mom and I want you to know that we accept and love you. Whether you are a little girl or a little boy, you are wanted by us. By the Holy Spirit, Jesus is there with you in your mother's womb, so you have nothing to be afraid of. God's love surrounds you. You will soon be getting ready to leave your present world to come into a new one and meet us, your mom and dad [add others here if appropriate]. Remember Jesus' presence is with you to protect you and bring you to us. He will also be with the doctor [midwife] to help him.
>
> Don't be afraid when the water breaks, because that opens the way to your birth and coming to us. The pressure won't seriously hurt you, although you may feel that it will; it's just bringing you to a new world and to us. We are eagerly waiting for you and will see you soon! You'll know us, because you've been listening to our voices for some time now. I love you. We love you. Jesus bless you!

A "Reliving the Scene With Jesus" Prenatal and Birth Meditation

Here's a meditation written by a member of the late Doris Smith's class at Bethlehem Baptist Church in Lake Oswego, Oregon. I've added some paragraphs on the end (after the break in the text). Be sure the person has scriptural preparation and is aware that Jesus' presence is there with him or her as early memories are dealt with. You will need to change the facts to fit the situation. Help the person see himself at his beginning, as far back as he can visualize.

Imagine yourself enveloped within what seems to be a self-sustaining system. Nutrients flow in to your body. Oxygen and carbon dioxide change equally. You are warm in a weightless suspension.

You've been there since our Lord placed your spirit within a woman's tiny egg at the moment it was fertilized by a specific man's sperm.

You choose when to sleep and when to be awake. Sometimes you choose to play, bouncing against the uterine walls of your mother. Sometimes you drink fluid; other times you spit it out. Sometimes you suck your thumb. Sometimes you kick your feet; other times you rest.

Listen to her heartbeat now; it comes through the pulse of her arteries. You know that heartbeat. You've been hearing it for some time.

For some all is well. Others of you can sense a lack, a general uneasiness. Maybe there's not enough oxygen. Perhaps the food supply is restricted. Sometimes your mental awareness is dulled. Even now you're being affected by your mother's anxieties, her inner struggles, her fears. And you're being affected by her joys, her carefulness, and all that life means to her.

Now something is happening. A wave of pressure sweeps over your body. The steady heartbeat you've come to know quickens. You sense an excitement. Is it expectant and joyful? Or is it fearful? It passes and you go back to your normal activities.

Then something new. Your little inner world is changing. Your buoyancy is altered, and another wave of pressure sweeps over you. Again the quickened pulse rate. You sense that your existence, as you know it, is about to be interrupted.

Another wave. What is happening? Why is your world changing? Yet another wave. The pressure increases. Why? Do you have any control over this?

Can you feel the pressure on your head as you are propelled down a course too narrow for your acceptance? Do you resist and pull back? Or do you allow yourself to be pushed further along? Do you have the urge to stop everything and gain control?

Why are you being forced from the home you know into a narrow passageway leading to who knows where? Why is God allowing this? Will He be on the other side? Or is He here all along and in your panic you have not heard His voice or felt His touch?

The pressure increases. It is incredible, but it is not unbearable. Can you see yourself in the dark birth canal and know that something new is happening to your body? Can you feel it?

Now your back and arms and legs and tummy begin to tingle and awaken—a new wave of pressure as if new life is being pumped into them. You see light at the end of the tunnel. Another wave and suddenly pressure on your head is at its greatest. Then the pressure stops. Your head is free. Then there's more pressure on your shoulders and now you have full freedom. . . .

Battle weary, you're caught by the doctor's (or somebody else's) hands; you're glad to see Jesus is standing close by.

As your umbilicus is cut I pray, "Dear Jesus, breathe the gift of life into these lungs You've created. Take away the pain of his [or her] first breath with your healing love."

As Jesus picks you up and holds you: "God, please heal this little one from whatever shock or pain he [or she] may have received at birth from coldness; vertigo; eye, back, ankle and ear pain, and any negative effect this might have on his [or her] attitudes in life."

Jesus' healing hands and love are making you whole. As your eyes look into His, the two of you are bonded in deep love forever. Jesus loves you so much and is proud of this tiny baby. It's obvious that you are just what He wanted.

"Dear Lord, please wash away any false guilt of feeling responsible for his mother's birth pains or any other serious complications she had at birth or following."

As Jesus holds you, visualize your parents and thank them for their part in bringing you into existence. If there's any particular reason to do so, forgive them, and if you can, see yourself being held and approved of by your mother and your father. See yourself receiving your first drink of good, sweet milk.

If you were separated from your mother for any extended period of time, "Dear God, please heal [*name*] from any feeling of loneliness or rejection. As the healing comes, help him feel more love for his mother."

Know that with Jesus with you everything is going to be just fine.

Other matters to pray about in the important first two years of the person's life:

If he was unduly left hungry or wet, or in pain, needing to be burped;

If he was deprived of his mother's love, or it wasn't given long enough or frequently enough to establish his own capacity to love;

If the characteristic of trust wasn't allowed to develop in the first or second year;

If at the end of eighteen months, when he should have begun to see himself as a separate person from the mother, he or she wasn't allowed to.

For the child who is a little older, you might ask him to draw and color a picture showing how he feels when in an unhappy place. This helps him express his emotions. Asking the child to talk about the picture also helps. Then it's good to have him or her include Jesus in the scene and tell how the picture changes.

An Example of Prayer

The following is an example of inner-healing prayer recorded by a young woman:

I stated to the counselors that I hated my mother for not loving me. I spoke forgiveness to my mother and asked God to forgive me. Then we asked Jesus to allow me to see how He meant my mother to be through praying a Creative Prayer.

First, Jesus held me really close and I could feel His love. Then He handed me to my mother, and she showered my face with kisses. I really liked this. Then she touched my hands, and I wrapped my fingers around her finger. Then she unwrapped my blanket and touched my legs and feet and stroked me all over. She then nursed me. I didn't want to stop nursing, but I was getting too full. One of the counselors said that the supply would be there whenever I wanted it, that I didn't have to take it all now. I was glad she said that. My mother continued to hold me close, and I dozed off and on for quite a while. Then Jesus took me and held me and burped me. I was glad He did, because I felt better physically right away. He then took me back to the nursery.

Feelings: The nursing desire had the same feeling that my present need for holding has. I feel ashamed that I wanted nursing so much. I also felt at birth that mother didn't want to hold me. She was afraid of such a fragile infant. Also I wondered if her reticence was that she wanted a boy first.

Forgiveness from the scene: I forgave mother if she did want a boy first. I forgave her for smoking and cutting off air supply at times.

I forgave her when the umbilical cord wrapped around my neck, for I may have blamed this on her somehow, since I as an infant wouldn't have understood where the choking feeling came from.

I asked forgiveness of God for my reaction to these hurts connected with my mother.

I asked His forgiveness for my hating my mother.

Observation: At the beginning of the prayer, when I began to hug one of the counselors, the Creative Prayer was blocked. I then realized that I couldn't go to others for comfort if I wanted the mother-daughter relationship to be healed. I really do want to be healed.

Overwhelming Need to Be Hugged

An insatiable desire to be held and hugged is usually due to a deprivation of love from one or both parents early in life, perhaps from birth. This inordinate craving for physical affection can be dealt with by God through soul-healing prayer, although it may take time. Through Creative Prayer, the counselee can receive the needed holding and loving from Jesus and the parent who was unable to give it. The prayer partners may hug the counselee to help and encourage, but normally it should be both of them together, not just one. They're trying to draw the counselee to Jesus, not to themselves.

A Testimony

Following is an interesting letter from Ada Hyde, Orange, California.

I was born in a small coal mining town in South Eastern Kentucky and we moved away when I was about four months old. Yet I always had the feeling of being home when we went back to visit when I was older. I remember a longing to always be there when there was a problem in my life. I felt if I could be there I would be safe, and nothing or no one could hurt me. When we went to visit, I would automatically wake up at 5:00 AM, before the whistle at the mines went off or the connecting of the first coal trains clanked together.

Years later, when there were no more trains or whistles when we went to visit, I would still wake up at the same time and go downstairs and sit on my Aunt Mary's front porch in the swing with such a peace that I never felt anyplace else in the world. I would wonder why my parents had left such a wonderful place and all the relatives who seemed to care so much.

I prayed for years for the Lord to let me go there to live before I died.

Then I attended a seminar at Melodyland. I wasn't at all sure about the idea of prenatal prayer. During the last day prayer was being offered from the time of conception. When it got to the part about the unborn baby beginning to hear, I suddenly heard train whistles and running water, and knew the Lord was showing me what I had heard and felt in the womb.

As the days went by, I began to understand why the longing to be in that town had been there. Those sounds were the first ones I heard all safe and secure in my mother's womb, where the Lord had covered me with His hand (Psalms 139:13). I also began to realize that wherever I am the Lord is, and I can now be at home anyplace!

There are many more examples I could give, but I need to finish this book! In this chapter, you and I have taken a journey to the beginning and have seen God there. "In the beginning, God." It's been an adventure, praying about things we never thought about before. It's such great joy to help a person see and experience God's love and care from the earliest moments of life. Not only that, but our prayers are the means by which God moves in the world.

God wants to heal the members of Christ's Body, making us more effective channels of healing in an unhealed world. All of us are needed for this work. Life's beginning may be a good place to begin!

I will instruct you and train you in the
way you shall go; I will counsel you with
My eye on you.

Psalms 32:8 MLB

8
You Don't Travel Alone

It takes courage for a pastor to let people begin sharing in the
ministry in such things as prayer-counseling. More and more, the
minister is realizing, though, that he can't possibly meet the needs
of the congregation, seeing them in church only a few hours each
week, and there just isn't enough of him to go around, even for
those who are brave enough to ask for personal attention.

The Beginnings of a New Ministry

Before Dennis resigned (after twenty-one years) from being rector (chief pastor) of Saint Luke's Episcopal Church in the spring of
1981 to pursue his outreach ministry, lay prayer-counseling had
been going on for three years. I was working in leadership in the
soul-healing ministry of the parish during those first three years. It
was a pioneering time, and a wonderful experience. As people were
helped, they told their friends, and soon we saw the need for a regular counselor-training program.

In 1978, Dennis and I began presenting our first seminars on
"Healing the Whole Person" at Saint Luke's, and out of this developed more teams of prayer-counselors. We began to teach a counselor's class prior to each seminar, and those who attended
benefited by in-service training at the seminar under the leadership
of those more experienced. We called the experienced persons *team
leaders* and the trainees *apprentices*. The four-hour classes and the
seven hours of teachings at the seminars, plus the two-and-one-

half to three-hour supervised prayer sessions, didn't fully qualify the trainees for leadership, but they were certainly on their way! Those who wanted to go into a church-sponsored inner-healing ministry needed further preparation.

Some didn't like putting the counselors into these two categories, but we were dealing with people's lives, and I felt the need to be sure they were prepared for this responsibility. We required that an apprentice counselor, after attending the training class and seminar, work under the direction of a team leader. In order to become a team leader, the person in training was to have shared in the prayer-counseling of at least three people to a successful conclusion, involving at least three meetings with each. If the team leader still felt he was not quite ready, he might be asked to train longer. Some, even after successfully completing the requirements, would themselves decide they needed more supervised experience.

When the apprentice and the team leader both believed he was ready, they, together with the director of inner-healing counseling, and the coordinator (roles explained later) would go to the pastor for his approval. If the pastor felt the person satisfied the requirements (chapter 2), he would appoint him or her to be a team leader, and he or she would begin to function in that capacity.

Canon Bruce Shortell, pastor of lay-counseling ministry at the Cathedral of Saint Philip, Atlanta, tells me that they commission counselors for inner healing at a Sunday-morning worship service, an excellent way for the church to affirm lay ministry.

The number of counselors has been maintained or increased at Saint Luke's through the five years since 1978, largely because, as we've said, two people work together. Not all team leaders feel called to train apprentices, but those who do continue to help new people grow into leadership.

Mary Carol Hansen, wife of the rector, and in leadership of prayer-counseling at Saint Stephen's Church, Gilroy, California, writes,

> We've learned some valuable lessons in the counseling ministry here, namely, not to give too much authority too soon to our counseling teams. . . . I read recently that "fidelity requires psychological strength" and that makes a lot of sense. The needs are so great and so deep in the persons God is bringing that it seems to require some

maturity and stability among the counselors. God is just working that in us now.

Mary Carol is so right. This is why we feel an apprenticeship program (or whatever you want to call it) is so important. It also helps to determine if a person who wants to serve is truly called to this particular ministry. Perhaps he or she would do better in evangelism, Sunday school, a specialized ministry in physical-healing prayer, administration, private intercession, and so forth.

Speaking for ourselves, during those final three years of Dennis's leadership at Saint Luke's, he did not have one complaint about the prayer-counselors or their work. The parish, which was already warm and loving, became tangibly more so. The church seemed to become more alive and caring. Without urging from the pastors, one night each week the Sunday-school classrooms were lighted and busy with twenty or more prayer-counselors praying for those in need. (In addition they prayed on other days at the church, and also in their homes.) This was exciting to us as pastor and wife.

Your Pastor Needs You and You Need Your Pastor

If you want to work with others outside your own immediate family in soul-healing ministry, the only safe way to do this is with the direction and blessing of your pastor. Excluding the professionally trained, those who launch out on their own, without guidance and fellowship, are highly vulnerable and I strongly advise against it.

You may say, "But my church leaders don't even understand inner-healing prayer, much less lay ministry." Then talk to your pastor and give him some literature. If he is open, have him get in touch with other pastors who have this work in their churches. (Some are listed in the back of *Emotionally Free,* and in the back of this book also.) If another church in your area has already stepped out in this field, perhaps its members will allow you to train and work under their supervision for a time. One of these days you might be asked to help establish this ministry in your own church.

This is the way we handled it while I was directing the program at Saint Luke's: if a person from another church came seeking training, we sent a form letter to his or her pastor for approval and blessing. Handling things this way also let the pastor know we weren't trying to steal his sheep! If he approved, the person was trained and worked with us for a time as a prayer-counselor. In the long run, it would mean great blessing to him and his church.

Even if you cannot yet find a place where you can be trained or serve, you and a good friend can read, pray, and grow in prayer ministry for yourselves and your own families. If other friends are interested, encourage them to pray within their own families until a door opens for wider ministry.

Organizing Prayer-Counseling Ministry in a Church

The Director. Someone should be appointed by the pastor to have general supervision of prayer-counseling. He should be accountable to the pastor and report to him at intervals. If he has a committee working with him, in this case, his or her title may be "chairman" or "chairperson."

The director, with the concurrence of the pastor, appoints a *coordinator* who will work closely with him or her.

The Coordinator. The coordinator may be a woman who does not have a job away from home; or it may be someone on the church staff, clergy or lay, or a retired man or woman who has the time to give, or someone hired by the church especially for the task.

This person needs to have a mind for details, to be compassionate, and to enjoy working with people. He or she must have a working knowledge of referral agencies in the area.

The coordinator is in charge of taking requests for counseling that come in, mostly by telephone. (In a busy church office, it is sometimes best to use the coordinator's home-telephone number, making less work for the church secretary.)

The coordinator needs to keep in touch with the prayer-counselors and their schedules and have a card box of their names and phone numbers by the telephone at all times. He also maintains a list of the people who may be waiting for help. (From time to time, this list may need to be temporarily closed, if overloaded.) He must estimate how many people can be helped by the number of prayer-counselors available, the extent of counseling need, and approximate length of time likely to be required.

An *active* prayer-counselor's list should be kept by the coordinator updated and given to the director (or chairman) and pastor every three months. Either the coordinator or active counselors need to submit monthly or bimonthly a report of ministry activities to the supervising priest or minister. This is a general report, and confidential details must be kept that way unless the coordinator and the counselee have had to visit the pastor for consultation.

The coordinator should himself have a working knowledge of soul-healing prayer-counseling, so he or she can effectively relate counselees to counselors. It is good if he can now and then work as a prayer-counselor, as time permits.

The coordinator must be objective enough not to take on the burdens of the people calling for help. It is important for the coordinator not to undertake more than he can handle. If the work grows too big, he, with the director's agreement, should choose a coworker. He must limit the hours he can be reached by telephone. It would be to the church's advantage to provide the coordinator with a telephone answering device, as it would mean less calls to the church office and would assist the coordinator too. (Since this entire effort, director, coordinator, and prayer-counselors, is given without charge to the church, most vestrymen or church boards and pastors should be only too happy to assist with such helps.)

Some people may complain, "All this is just making more work for our church!" To that I reply, "Isn't one of the church's major missions to heal the brokenhearted and emotionally bruised?" If you must plan how to help those coming to your church for prayer healing, be thankful, because it means you have problems of life and not death. Too often in the past, those in need have felt the church was the *last* place to go when they needed real help.

Director's Further Duties

In addition to overall supervision, the director needs to plan monthly support meetings for counselors. This is so the counselors can have fellowship and continue to grow. You may have a report on a particular book in the field or one related to it; a prayer workshop; have a series of teachings led by team leaders in fields of special expertise which they have developed; invite a special speaker; invite the pastor to share; and so forth. Team leaders and apprentices should make it a priority and commitment to attend these monthly support meetings.

I always enjoyed planning a yearly mini-retreat held for one day in a downtown hotel, usually with a guest speaker invited. I suggest you do the same. Often you can find a motel or hotel that has a free conference room, if you order a catered lunch. Team leaders and active apprentices are invited. The church may want to subsidize the expense.

In the summer, I found it a good idea to have six weekly public meetings with team leaders for speakers. This helped to get the church, and others who came, acquainted with new capable prayer-counselors, so the better-known ones didn't have too many demands made on them. These meetings were very popular and effective, and when the word got out, people came from many other churches. (Realize such meetings will bring you more requests for prayer help!).

Some Questions Answered

1. *How does a prayer-counselor keep from being worn out by counseling sessions?*

I can only speak from my experience. Others may of course find it different.

I find this kind of counseling does not deplete my energy as other kinds did in the past. This is because I'm relying on the Holy Spirit's guidance, and Jesus is the center and focal point of what is happening. Also, I have a prayer partner with whom to share the load.

Then, too, I don't come to listen to a person rehearse all his past sins leaving me with heaviness. Remember that inner healing focuses on healing the result of sins committed by *others* against us, and in contrast, confession and God's imparted forgiveness heals the sins *we* have committed against others. As I've said already, both may be involved but prayer-counseling is *mainly healing hurts caused by others.*

2. *How do you handle it when a person drops in unexpectedly, in the middle of a meal, asking for prayer?*

I would determine if it was a real emergency, and if so, I would call my prayer partner, and if possible, we would meet with the counselee. I would let the person know that in the future, he or she should call on the phone first, since I need to give my family priority.

If it wasn't an emergency, I would give the person a cup of tea, a magazine to read, excuse myself, and finish dinner with my family. Afterwards, I would talk to the counselee for ten or fifteen minutes and point out that further counseling must wait until our next regular session together.

3. *How do you keep prayer-counselors from being overworked with too many counselees?*

The coordinator comes in here; work through him (or her). Instead of people coming to you directly, you should encourage them to work through the coordinator. If you are a well-known and effective counselor, people will probably contact you directly and that makes it harder to say *no.* You should determine how many people you can work with without overtiring yourself, or taking needed time away from your family, and stick to that quota. Learn to say, "I'd like to, but I can't."

Another possible solution is to concentrate part of your counseling time training others.

4. *What if some of the people in my church don't want to be prayed with by those of their own fellowship?*

This is why it's good to have other churches involved, so you can work together. A coordinator at one church can contact a coordinator at a nearby church, so they may trade counselees.

5. *What if I make a mistake in counseling? What should I do?*

We want to do the best job possible—that's why we don't take preparation time lightly. Working in twos also has a "checks and balances" feature to it. However, no one is perfect. If a mistake is made, talk it over with the director, do what you can to rectify the mistake, receive prayer help if you need it, and release the problem to the Lord. I like what the Reverend John Powell says in *The Secret of Staying in Love:* "The only real mistake is the one from which we learn nothing."

6. *What should I do if a person offers me money because he appreciates my help so much?*

Lovingly decline. You may suggest he instead offer a gift to your church, or whichever church has sponsored your training. Sometimes counselees will bring you berries from their vines, vegetables from their gardens, or remember some special occasion with a purchased gift. These things you may accept. The counselee needs to realize that such gifts are not in any way expected. One of the great things about lay counseling is that the counselee realizes it's done strictly out of love—no strings attached.

Dr. Margery Terpstra, psychotherapist in Honolulu, Hawaii, makes this comment in reference to training lay counselors in a letter to me:

> I believe that people can be taught to help themselves, and then to help others, and so the good news can spread. However, there are some eager-to-be helpers who get people into more self-examination and recalling of hurts than they are able to handle. Therefore, I feel most comfortable with extended training sessions. Some individuals, who may not yet be equipped with either spiritual or natural gifts, need to sort through their own lives before they are encouraged to "help" others.

This is a word of caution we should remember. Though some groups may, we aren't urging self-examination for the sins of counselees, though if they come up spontaneously during the course of prayer, they will then be dealt with. When it comes to remembering hurts of the past, it's so important to pray for the Holy Spirit to surface the needs to pray about. We aren't qualified to be "diggers" into a person's life, but with patience and prayer, the work will be safely and effectively done. (Please refer to my last chapter in *Emotionally Free* pages 232–235 and the list of Six Cautions.)

Remember too:

Inner-healing prayer can't be used as a substitute
for repentance
nor is
repentance a substitute for inner-healing prayer.

If, after weeks of healing prayer, a person isn't willing to repent from his own wrong attitudes when they are clearly and gently revealed, then you won't get anywhere, and you will know that your time is being wasted. It's helpful to see where our hurts originated, so those relationships can be healed, but that's no excuse to blame parents or anyone else in the future. Remember, too, that when there are hurts to pray about, you shouldn't simply be scouting around to find some "secret sin" causing the problems, but get on with loving and praying for the person's memories.

A friend of mine, Judi Howell, in Jacksonville, Florida, who has a fruitful prayer-counseling ministry under the headship of a fine clergyman has this to say:

> Because of what God has done in my life I was asked to give my testimony in many places. I prayed with hundreds of people for healing and saw many miracles. I guess I needed a balance to keep me from a case of "glory be to me" and that began when God led me into another kind of ministry. (I still do the other, too, as led.)
>
> I have to tell you that prayer-counseling is truly a "Back Room" service. It is usually all day, and many times there are many sessions. I must say this has been the most rewarding overall experience in my walk with Jesus.
>
> To have the privilege of being an instrument God uses to see His children released from all sorts of bondage, teaching and participating in the healing that comes with forgiveness, is fantastic! To be allowed to see Jesus heal painful memories, and to walk back to the womb experience, and then through a troubled childhood to the present, is a miracle. He wants to come into *every* damaging, hurtful situation. It is so obvious to me that we are all products of our past, and knowing we can be set free is tremendously exciting to me. I know that this is totally a ministry of love, self-sacrifice, and healing. I think that because of all of the healing I needed and received, the Lord lets me minister to others in this capacity.

Never Alone

No, you don't travel alone in this ministry of prayer. You travel under the guidance and direction of God: Father, Son, and Holy Spirit; with the leadership of godly pastors who "watch out for your souls"; and in fellowship with a large number of laity, clergy, and professional therapists who feel a call to this ministry. Let's walk hand in hand, growing and learning together.

I trust that you now feel you've received definite direction for praying for soul healing for yourself and others. I've given you many practical examples in this book as well as in *Emotionally Free,* but I've tried to share a concept more than a method: the concept of Jesus as the omnipresent Healer—past, present and future. He loves you unconditionally and wants to make you whole: spirit, soul, and body. And He wants to work through His Body on earth to establish His kingdom.

> If we shouldn't expect healing on earth,
> and we don't need it in heaven,
> then what is it for?

Obviously, it's for now. Put your life more and more into the healing hands of Jesus, and with joy bring others to Him, who is the source of all wholeness.

Epilogue
You're Part of the Cure

I have been asked, "Does the ministry of soul-healing (or inner-healing) prayer take into consideration the crucified life?"

The "crucified life" is basic to Christianity—the foundation upon which we build; yet few explain what they mean when they talk about it. The crucified life has nothing to do with self-torment. It doesn't mean that life should be a continuous crucifixion! It's not trying to get rid of yourself. It's not wearing a hair shirt, or scourging yourself, as some did in the Middle Ages.

The Crucified Life

Arnold Walker from Natal, South Africa, produces a devotional guide, *Faith for Daily Living*. In the July 1981 issue, he describes the crucified life:

> ... True Christianity is a way of life empowered by God's Holy Spirit, that will enable you to become so closely identified with the Living Christ that you eventually think His thoughts and perform His actions. To be identified with Christ should be the goal of every Christian.
>
> Such close liaison with Christ must not be attempted lightly or thoughtlessly, for though you may experience deep satisfaction, great joy, and continuing peace as you draw nearer to Him, you will also become acutely aware of the needs of your fellowmen. The agony of the human family, with its hatreds, divisions, starvation, bitterness, greed, and other symptoms of imperfection, will press in upon you as you seek to serve Him who loves all people.
>
> To be identified with Christ means that you are no longer part of the sickness of the world but have become a part of its cure. You will annul hatred by love; overcome evil with good; and acknowledge the supremacy of the Spirit of Christ over the destructive spirit of a Christless world.

I would like to add:

If you're working at forgiving everyone, as the Lord's Prayer indicates you should,

If you continue to reach out with open arms while being rejected,

If you care enough about others so that you can forget about yourself, listen to them, pray with them, and sometimes care for them physically,

If you attempt to live and love as Jesus said,

You are living the crucified life.

If you love your neighbor as yourself, even though he plays loud music or keeps measuring the property line,

If you keep loving your mate, forgiving seventy times seven, and praying when part of you says you should give up,

If your child is living immorally, or is on drugs, but you keep loving, praying, and forgiving,

If you are trying to show the unconditional love of Jesus, while others believe such love impossible,

That's the crucified life.

I see this kind of life expressed in and through soul-healing ministry. Anyone who is doing this kind of praying is to some extent walking in the crucified life, and helping others to do so. It seems to me that praying for others for the healing of their souls shows this kind of life through giving time with patience and love. And as people are healed in their souls, they too are set free to live the crucified life.

It's a Fact

As I understand from Scripture, when you are born again, or regenerated, your *spirit* which was "dead in sins" is cleansed, and resurrected from the dead, becoming a new creature. It is washed in the water of God's Word, cleansed by the blood of Jesus, and born into God's family (Titus 3:5–7; 1 Peter 1:18, 19; 1 Peter 1:23; John 3:7).

Your *soul* or psychological nature is also cleansed, and the "old man" (or what we inherited from Adam) dealt with through identification with our crucified Lord Jesus. Yet, from Scripture we see that the soul is still in the process of being made holy, or sanctified (Romans 6:6; 11–13). The old nature is removed, but habit patterns that were established still need to be dealt with as they assert themselves. "Stinking thinking," wrong emotional responses, wrong physical habits, must be submitted to the life-changing power of the Holy Spirit.

What does it mean to say with Paul, "I am crucified with Christ . . ." (Galatians 2:20)? Some have taught that when you accept Jesus, you cease to exist. Well meaning as it may be, this "annihilation" concept has often created feelingless people who are more like machines than human beings. A friend of mine visited a group who were trying so hard to crucify the "old man" that they sat at dinner, and for an hour or so afterwards in the living room, in silence, speaking only if they were going to talk about something "spiritual." Such questions as, "How's your family?" or, "What have you been doing lately?" were strictly unacceptable! They were sincere people, but such asceticism will not bring about the desired results.

In Galatians, Paul says, "I am crucified with Christ: nevertheless I live; yet not I, but Christ liveth in me: and the life which I now live in the flesh I live by the faith of the Son of God, who loved me, and gave himself for me" (2:20 KJV). To understand what Paul means, you need to look at Jesus' words and life. Jesus didn't say, "I don't exist; it's only My Father who exists." He said, "Before Abraham was, I am!" "I am the way," "I am the door," "I am the true vine." But He always deferred to His Father. He did exactly what His loving Father showed Him and what would please His Father.

"I am crucified with Christ. Yet I live." Yes, I am an individual person with a unique personality loved by God. God and I have been joined together Spirit to spirit. (1 Corinthians 6:17). We're joined as one spirit; yet God is a Person (tri-Personal, yet One) and I am a person. I'm not, as some religions teach, swallowed up in the "all." I am. I exist—yet I don't want to see myself apart from God, any more than Jesus wanted to see Himself apart from His Father.

God is in me, and that's the greatest of all mysteries! (Read Colossians 1:26, 27.)

Paraphrased, the Galatians 2:20 passage might read like this:

> I am (spirit and soul) crucified with Christ. Nevertheless I (the reborn me) live, yet not I alone but Christ lives in me (lives in my spirit, touching my soul and body, as I allow Him to). And the life I now live in this physical body, I live by the faith of Jesus, God's only begotten Son, who loved me and gave Himself for me.

Life Out of Death

I am crucified, *yet I live.* Crucifixion brings *resurrection.* Crucifixion isn't something we do to ourselves. If you're a Christian, that crucifixion is an accomplished fact. If you are living in Christ, you are living the crucified life. Self-denial is different in that you still need to yield your will to God daily (Matthew 16:24). But you accomplish this best by looking at the numerous good things God has for you rather than on the negative *I can'ts.* Now you can concentrate on the positive aspects of resurrection life, as you walk in the Spirit, and God will be able to change you from the inside out.

"If then you were raised with Christ, seek those things which are above, where Christ is, sitting at the right hand of God. Set your mind on things above, not on things on the earth. For you died [the old you], and your life [new resurrection life] is hidden with Christ in God" (Colossians 3:1–3).

Accept the fact that you have been crucified with Christ. Consider it done (Romans 6:11). And now live the resurrected life, doing the work Jesus called you to do.

Yes, You're Part of the Cure!

Each soul-healing prayer is an encounter with the resurrected Lord Jesus. Through such encounters, you and those you pray with become more and more like Him. You want to do what He wants you to do: to share the Good News of God's great love; to heal the sick; bind up the bruised and brokenhearted; set captives free; open prison doors in the soul—give sight and insight to the spiritually blind; comfort those who mourn; give them oil of joy, beauty for ashes, and garments of praise for spiritual heaviness. Break every yoke (Isaiah 61:1, 3; 58:6; Luke 4:18; Psalms 142:7).

You've identified with Christ. You're not a part of the sickness of the world, but *part of the cure.* This is the crucified life, and, yes, this is the resurrection life.

Appendix 1

A Suggested Form of Prayer for Receiving Jesus as Savior

Dear Jesus, I believe You are God's only begotten Son, come in human flesh. I believe You died on the cross, and poured out Your life's blood to wash away the sins of the world. I believe You rose from the dead, physically, to give a new kind of life.

I confess my sins to You—all the wrong things I have done. I ask You to forgive me, and wash me in Your precious blood. I believe You are doing that right now. Thank you for cleansing me. I receive Your forgiveness.

I open the door of my life to You. Come in, Lord Jesus. Come and live in me. I receive You as My Savior and Lord. I believe You have come into my spirit and have given me resurrection life. I believe You're living in me by the Holy Spirit, and I'm born again. I have received Your new kind of life! Thank You, Jesus! I love You, Lord, and will walk with You all my days. *Amen.*

(For further assistance in knowing how to lead someone to Christ, read the first two chapters of our book *The Holy Spirit and You,* or get the handy booklet *Four Spiritual Laws* by Bill Bright of Campus Crusade for Christ International, Arrowhead Springs, San Bernardino, CA 92414.

Mark these verses of Scripture: Romans 3:23; 5:8; 6:23; Gospel of John 1:12; 2 Corinthians 5:17; Revelation 3:20.

Prayer for the Adopted

A minister friend who has worked with adopted children and has an adopted child of his own, says that they are born with a sense of rejection far beyond what they consciously understand. This subconscious emotion may cause them to struggle for approval or, on the other hand, to act in antisocial ways.

I think it's best in praying for the adopted to simply go back and pray from the time of conception through their birth. Prepare them by explaining that Jesus is always present. You might share with them the Scriptures about conception, prenatal life, and birth as I've given in chapter 7, "Journey to Life's Beginning."

The time to pray for a child, with his conscious participation, is when he begins to question you about being adopted. For a child, give him one Scripture at a time and talk about what each one means; this will help him be ready for prayer. Little children like to see pictures of babies and there are beautiful pictures of children before birth in the book *A Child Is Born.* If you think it would be helpful, share these pictures about the beginning of life with the adopted child before praying.

If the birth was out of wedlock *and the person knows it,* I remind him Jesus was there at his conception and whether anybody else wanted him or not, Jesus did, and rejoiced. The person may speak forgiveness to the parents for their mistakes, and at the same time be thanking God for the gift of life and that "all things work together for good." A child may want to make a prayer such as this when older.

Another prayer both adult and child may be guided to pray is: "Dear Father, I give up all the hurts I've suffered from the time I lived in my mother's womb until now. In Jesus' name."

Now you may pray the Creative Prayer in chapter 11 of *Emotionally Free* or your own modification of it. Pray any of the other soul-healing prayers as needed.

Prayer for the Elderly

There are two major things which trouble the older person: one, that he doesn't feel needed any longer; and two, that he may become dependent again as in his childhood. There are more opportunities for hurts in childhood and in old age than at any other time in life. It may help to remember that the person inside the older body doesn't feel as old as his body looks. In fact, he's the same person but can't function as he or she once did.

The older a person lives to be, the more memories there are to think about. He usually remembers the past more easily than the present. If his early memories are good, great; if bad, then they need to be prayed for. A person is never too old to pray about his earliest times. You may pray Reliving the Scene With Jesus Prayers, or Creative Prayers, according to need.

Appendix 2

How to Lead Someone in Renouncing the Cults or the Occult:

Dear Father, if I have believed, or read, or taught, or taken part in anything that was contrary to Your Word, or displeasing to You, in Jesus' name I renounce those acts or thoughts, and especially [*here mention the specifics that need to be renounced*]. I promise You I will not engage in these anymore, and that I will destroy any literature, equipment, or symbols associated with these things at my earliest opportunity.

Any spirits associated with any of these, in Jesus' name, I bind you and command you to depart from me and trouble me no more. I renounce you, Satan, and all your works. Jesus, I confess You as my Lord and I thank You for giving Your life for me. I claim the protection of Your precious blood as I pray. Thank You, Jesus.

After the person has prayed this way, *you* pray for him or her, and ask God to fill with His Holy Spirit any areas left vacant. It would be good to have the counselee pray, too, "Lord Jesus, I ask You to fill my life with Your Holy Spirit that I may walk with You in Your truth and light. Thank You, Lord."

(For further information on this see our book *The Holy Spirit and You*, chapters 4, 5, and 12; and *Emotionally Free*, chapter 15.)

Appendix 3

List of Churches with Active Soul/Inner-Healing Ministries

In the back of my book *Emotionally Free,* I listed some churches that have active soul/inner-healing ministries. Here are more to add to the list:

The Christain Center Church, Albuquerque, New Mexico. The Rev. Colin Wellard, Chief Pastor.

Saint Margaret's Episcopal Church, Belleview, Washington. The Rev. Wallace Bristol, Rector.

Episcopal Church of the Resurrection, Dallas, Texas. The Rev. Ted Nelson, Rector.

Saint David's Anglican Church, Delta, British Columbia, Canada. The Rev. Arthur Nash, Rector.

Colonial Bible Church, Federal Way, Washington. The Rev. Dave Engebretson, Chief Pastor.

Faith Lutheran Church, Geneva, Illinois. The Rev. Delbert R. Rossin, Chief Pastor, and The Rev. David M. Dorpat, Associate Pastor. Richard Fisk, director of inner-healing ministries.

Bethlehem Baptist Church, Lake Oswego, Oregon. The Rev. Jack Matthews, Lead Pastor, and Charles W. Moore, Pastor and counselor in charge of inner-healing ministries.

Devon United Church of Christ, Milford, Connecticut. The Rev. Howard MacMullen, Pastor.

Wildermere Beach United Church of Christ, Milford, Connecticut. The Rev. Hartford Inlow, Pastor.

Saint Stephen's Episcopal Church, Oak Harbor, Washington. The Rev. Jack Tench, Rector.

Saint John's Episcopal Church, Roseville, California. The Rev. Jerry W. Brown, Rector.

Saint Luke's Episcopal Church, Bath, Ohio. The Rev. Chuck Irish, Rector, and Mary Litzell, parish coordinator for inner-healing prayer.

Saint Michael's Episcopal Church, Wayne, New Jersey. The Rev. Fred Gutekunst, Rector.

Bibliography

Bennett, Dennis. *Moving Right Along in the Spirit.* Old Tappan, N.J.: Fleming H. Revell Company, 1983.

Bennett, Rita. *Emotionally Free.* Old Tappan, N.J.: Fleming H. Revell Company, 1982.

Bennett, Dennis and Rita. *The Holy Spirit and You.* Plainfield, N.J.: Bridge Publishers, 1971.

————. *Trinity of Man.* Plainfield, N.J.: Bridge Publishers, 1979.

Dobson, James. *Hide or Seek.* Old Tappan, N.J.: Fleming H. Revell Company Rev. Ed., 1974.

Dobson, Theodore E. *How to Pray for Spiritual Growth.* New York: Paulist Press, 1982.

Ingelman-Sundberg, Axel, and Wirsens, Claes. *A Child Is Born.* New York: Delacorte Press, Rev. Ed., 1977.

Leboyer, Frederick. *Birth Without Violence.* New York: Alfred A. Knopf, Inc., 1982.

MacNutt, Francis. *Healing.* Notre Dame, Indiana: Ave Maria Press, 1974.

O'Neill, Cherry Boone. *Starving for Attention.* New York: Continuum Publishing Company, 1982.

Osborne, Cecil. *Release From Fear and Anxiety.* Waco, Texas: Word Books, 1976.

Payne, Leanne. *The Broken Image.* Westchester, Ill.: Cornerstone Books, 1981.

Powell, John, S.J. *The Secret of Staying in Love.* Niles, Ill.: Argus Communications, 1974.

Verny, Thomas, M.D., and Kelly, John. *The Secret Life of the Unborn Child.* New York: Summit Books, 1981.

White, Anne S. *Trial by Fire.* Kirkwood, Mo.: Impact Books MO, 1975.